PUPPET PLAY

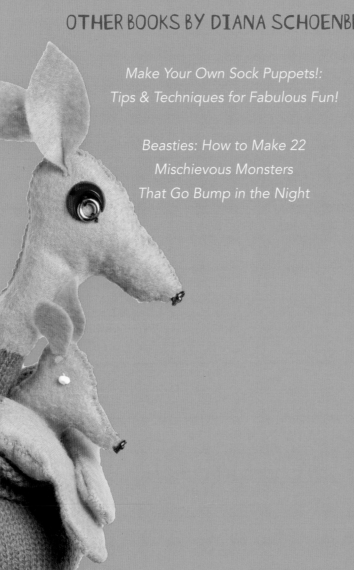

OTHER BOOKS BY DIANA SCHOENBRUN

Make Your Own Sock Puppets!:
Tips & Techniques for Fabulous Fun!

Beasties: How to Make 22
Mischievous Monsters
That Go Bump in the Night

PUPPET
PLAY

20 Puppet Projects Made with Recycled Mittens, Towels, Socks, and More!

Diana Schoenbrun

Photography by Tory Williams

Andrews McMeel Publishing, LLC

Kansas City • Sydney • London

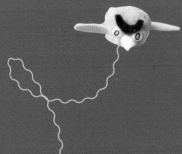

PUPPET PLAY

11 12 13 14 15 TEN 10 9 8 7 6 5 4 3 2 1

ISBN: 978-1-4494-0119-1

Library of Congress Control Number: 2010930541

Photography by Tory Williams, www.torywilliamsphotography.com.

Book design by Diane Marsh

Cover design by Julie Barnes

www.dianaschoenbrun.com

www.andrewsmcmeel.com

CONTENTS

INTRODUCTION

What do you do with a holey sock? Turn it into a magical wizard! What do you do with a sad glove that has lost its mate? Turn it into the five little pigs puppets! What do you do with that leg warmer stuffed in your drawer? Turn it into a crazy cat puppet!

In *Puppet Play* you'll discover how to make these fun puppets and many more for endless hours of crafting fun and family play. Each innovative puppet is made using recycled and reused materials that can be easily found around the home. You can use a variety of items for the body of the puppet, such as socks, gloves, mittens, scarves, towels, bandanas, and many other reusable household items. The function of an ordinary object changes by using your creativity and artistic eye. Then you add the details using thread, glue, felt, buttons, and more. Found objects from inside or outside your home can be transformed into amazing puppetry art. Best of all, you can create handmade personalized toys that you can animate.

These twenty do-it-yourself projects can be done alone or with the help of an adult or friend, depending on your age and ability. Each project has a level range from 1 to 3: level 1—beginner, 2—intermediate, and 3—advanced. First, you find your materials—a great way to introduce being green in a fun way. Then you cut, glue, and sew your way to adorable puppet creatures. After, it's time to practice your puppeteering skills, adding voice and movement to bring your puppet characters to life. You can even put on your own live puppet show by building a puppet stage! Puppets are popular in movies, television, and theater. Now you can create your very own handmade puppets and be puppeteer of the show!

PUPPET BUILDING AND MATERIALS

MAKING PUPPETS

To start making the puppets shown in the book, you may want to go on a treasure hunt through your house. Start with the sock drawer and dig up those holey ancient socks and the lonely socks that have lost their mates. Then peruse your drawers and find those retired mittens and gloves. Do you have leg warmers and scarves you have not worn in years? Does your closet contain a t-shirt that should be moved into the rag pile? Raid the linen closet for old washcloths and towels. Check the kitchen for a wooden spoon or empty can. Search in boxes, in bags, and under couch cushions for any other puppet accouterments you can find. Ask your family members for anything they don't want. If you still can't find enough to start with, then you can always go to the store to find accessories. The materials to make puppets are inexpensive and can be purchased at local discount, retail, and craft stores.

REUSED AND RECYCLED MATERIALS

Each project lists recycled and reused items at the beginning of the materials list. These are the primary reused objects needed for the puppet's body. Each project will list additional materials that may be found at home and reused or also can be purchased.

Here is a list of the reused objects you may use for the base of the puppet for projects in this book:

socks	leg warmers	cans
gloves	sweaters	cardboard egg cartons
mittens	t-shirts	cereal box cardboard
washcloths	dish and tea towels	
scarves	bandanas	

ADDITIONAL PUPPET PATTERNS

Here are some basic shapes you can use for additional eyes, ears, noses, and other parts to make with felt or fabric. You may need to enlarge them when photo-copying or scanning them.

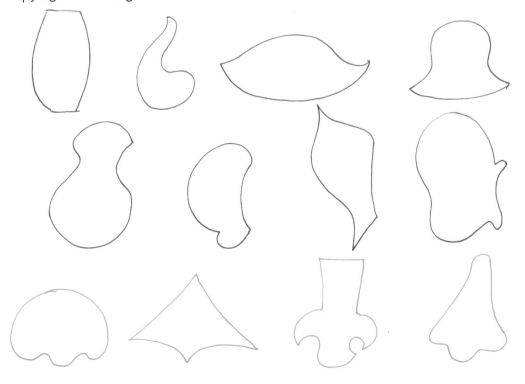

EMBELLISHMENTS

Many fabrics are great to use when making ears, eyes, noses, hair, and other accessories. Felt and fleece are easy to cut and use because they do not unravel or fray at the edges. Cotton, corduroy, and synthetic fabrics are fine too, but they are more likely to fray. Feel free to use different color fabrics than those suggested in the projects. Why not make a purple monkey or a green giraffe instead of the color shown?

Here are extra materials and decorations you may already have in your home; if not, they can easily be purchased. They will make your puppet unique.

- Pom poms come in all shapes and sizes and can be used for noses and eyes. Pom poms can be sewn or glued on.

- Pipe cleaners are great for structure. Sew or glue to an edge of an ear, tail, or leg. Pipe cleaners can easily be twisted and shaped.

- Googly eyes come in many shapes, sizes, and colors. Glue is necessary to attach them.

- Buttons can be used for eyes and noses.

- Ribbon and lace can add frill to your puppet.

- Popsicle sticks and straws are good for teeth and tusks.

- Egg cartons can be used for three-dimensional eyes.

- Beads, rhinestones, and glitter can be added with glue. Beads can also be sewn on.

- String and yarn are ideal for wigs.

- Faux fur makes awesome hair for your puppets, keeps them warm, and is perfect for characters with beards or mustaches.

- Stuffing such as polyfill, pantyhose, or fabric scraps can help fill out areas of your puppet to give it more shape.

Consider these other unique materials you may want to try: false eyelashes, play jewelry, vintage jewelry, doll clothes, shoelaces, barrettes, hair ties, twist ties, vegetable nets, bubble wands, bottle caps, balloons, feathers, key covers, washers, zippers, wire springs, notebook spirals, paper clips, erasers, paper towel or toilet paper rolls, clothes-pins, wooden spoons, paper cups, toothpicks, cotton swabs, chopsticks, wire hangers, fishing line, and more. Just use your imagination!

CONSTRUCTION MATERIAL AND TOOL LIST

Some of the following will be helpful for puppet construction.

ruler	embroidery needles	paint brushes
fabric scissors	pins	stuffing
fabric marker	pin cushion	wire cutters
chalk	thread	pliers
paper scissors	craft glue	sewing machine (optional)
sewing needles	hot glue gun	
embroidery floss	paint	

PUPPETMAKING SAFETY

Children should work with adults to be safe, especially when using hot glue guns, sharp scissors, and other tools such as wire cutters, pliers, or sewing machines. When making puppets for toddlers and younger children, use soft materials only, such as fabric and felt.

Help a child get started when using sewing needles or pins.

SEWING AND GLUING

CONSTRUCTING YOUR PUPPET

Many of the puppets need to be sewn together. If you don't have a sewing machine, do not fret. The projects in this book can all be made with a few simple hand stitches.

To prepare your needle, thread one strand of thread through the eye of the needle, pull it through, and fold it over so that you have a double thickness of thread with the needle at one end and the spool at the other. You'll have to guess at the length based on how far you're going to sew, but as a general rule, make your length of doubled-up thread at least twice as long as the length you need to sew. But don't make it more than 12 inches because the longer it is the easier it is to get tangled up. Cut the thread at the spool and tie a knot at the end of the two strands to keep it from pulling through the fabric as you sew.

You may want to use sewing pins to hold your fabric together while you sew. It may also help to use a washable fabric pen to mark a straight, even sewing line to follow. If you dab a little water on it later, the ink will disappear and only your straight stitches will show!

Running stitch (or straight stitch) is a simple straight stitch. Bring the threaded needle up through the back of the fabric about 1/4 inch from the edges of the fabric and pull it through until the knot catches at the back. You'll want to keep that distance from the edges even as you sew your line of stitches. Then bring the needle back down about 1/4 inch to the left or right (depending on which direction you like to sew) of where the thread first came up. Bring the needle up through the back again about 1/8 inch from where the thread came down, going in the same direction you did before. Repeat with your remaining stitches, keeping your over stitches even and making them longer than your under stitches.

Backstitch is a straight stitch that mimics a sewing machine stitch. Unlike the running stitch, where you keep sewing forward, the backstitch takes you back and forth, for a tighter line of overlapped (or nearly overlapped) stitches. Bring the threaded needle up from underneath the fabric about 1/4 inch from the edges of the fabric and pull it through until the knot catches at the back. You'll want to keep

that distance from the edges even as you sew your line of stitches. Then bring the needle back down about 1/4 inch to the left of where the thread came up. Bring the needle up again about 1/4 inch to the left of where the thread went down, then move your needle 1/4 inch to the right and push the needle down through the fabric where your previous top stitch ended. Bring your needle up 1/4 inch to the left of the last stitch in the row, backtrack again to the end of the last stitch, and keep repeating until you reach the end of the section you're sewing. You'll have a solid row of stitches on top and a solid row of long stitches on the back.

Whip stitch is used to attach two pieces of fabric by binding them together around the edges. Begin by inserting the needle into the fabric from the back about 1/4 inch from the fabric edges and pull it through until the knot catches at the back. You'll want to keep that distance from the edges even as you sew your stitches. Bring the needle up and then back down at a diagonal over the edges to the back side of the fabric. Bring the needle back through the fabric slightly to the right of the first spot where the thread came up. Wrap it back around the edges at a diagonal. Repeat, keeping your stitches evenly spaced, until you reach the end of the section you're sewing.

Cross-stitch is a simple repetition of diagonal stitches that are made by bringing the needle and thread up through the fabric in a row. Then the diagonal stitches are done in reverse in the opposite direction to make the X or cross.

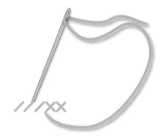

Blanket stitch is a visible stitch that is decorative and binds edges together. Begin by inserting the needle into the fabric from the back about 1/4 inch from the fabric edges and pull it through until the knot catches at the back. Bring the needle from the front and to the left, up to the desired height of your stitch and poke into the fabric, pulling the needle down and catching the trailing thread. Repeat stitches so they are evenly spaced.

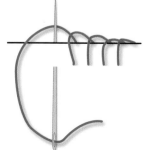

In certain projects you can use glue to attach puppet parts instead of sewing them. Either craft glue or hot glue will work. Hot glue guns do save time, but make sure to be careful when using them because they're very hot. You may want to ask an adult for help. Be careful not to touch the tip of the hot glue gun (or the hot glue!) and keep the hot glue gun plugged in only when needed.

Don't use too much of any type of glue or it will run and drip on your puppet. Certain craft glues or tacky glues can take only minutes to dry to the touch but longer to fully set, so you may have to wait a few minutes to complete a next step or to play with another finished puppet. Always read the specific directions on the glue bottle.

TAKING CARE OF YOUR PUPPET

You are the puppet maker, so take extra care of your craft! Perhaps your puppet took a liking to a late-night pizza feast or fell into a bowl of cereal at breakfast. No need to worry. A machine did not manufacture your puppet, so do not machine wash. Your puppet was made by hand, so wash it by hand. A spot scrub and a soak in the sink with detergent will do the trick.

Also, a reminder to pet owners: Most likely, your dog and cat will love your puppet as much as you do but may show their affection in another way—by chewing it! So please keep puppets out of reach from Fido and Fifi!

BANJO JILL

LEVEL 2

Throughout town you can hear Banjo Jill strumming sweetly on her little ole banjo. She learned to play from her uncle, Banjo Eddy, famous for shortening bread and hot licks. Jill frequents riverside hot spots especially before sunset. Her melodies hearken of the good times, the bad times, and all the times in between. At the county hoedown, Jill's friends join in on fiddle, harmonica, washboard, and jug.

MATERIALS

REUSED AND RECYCLED

1 dish towel or tea towel

1 scrap of colored cotton, wool, or felt for the face

1 scrap of denim, 1 1/2 x 2 1/2 inches

1 scrap of pink felt

1 piece of burlap, about 10 x 3 inches

white card stock

colored card stock

EMBELLISHMENTS

2 small beads

2 plastic pieces for the mouth (I used half-moons)

tiny shell

ball of jute twine

shoelace

large empty thread spool (about 1 3/4 inches high)

ribbon

junk metal or jewelry piece

small mixing wooden spoon

CONSTRUCTION MATERIALS AND TOOLS

ruler

fabric scissors

pins

sewing machine (optional)

sewing needle

thread in a color to match the dish or tea towel

black thread

craft glue

hot glue gun

pencil

CUT FROM PATTERN

FROM DISH/TEA TOWEL
2 body shapes

FROM COLORED COTTON
1 face shape

FROM WHITE CARD STOCK
1 banjo shape A

FROM COLORED CARD STOCK
1 banjo shape B

1 banjo shape C

1 banjo shape D

CUT FREEHAND

FROM PINK FELT
2 circles about the size of a dime

FROM BURLAP
2 squares, 3 x 3 inches

1 rectangle large enough to wrap around empty spool of thread

2

INSTRUCTIONS

1 Center the face shape on the head of one body shape, placing the wrong side of the face shape fabric against the right side of the body shape fabric. Pin in place. Machine sew a straight stitch or hand sew a running stitch or whip stitch around the edge of the face to attach it to the body.

2 Cut the denim piece in half so you have two pockets for the dress. Lay one full body piece right side up on your work surface. Place the pockets on the body and hand or machine sew around the side and bottom edges. Leave the top sides open and unsewn.

3 Place one side of your puppet right side up on your work surface. Place the other side right side down on top, matching edges, and pin together. Machine sew a straight stitch or hand sew a whip stitch about 1/4 inch from the edges around the body, starting at point A and continuing to point B, leaving the side for the hand opening unsewn.

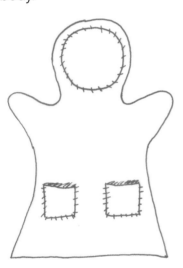

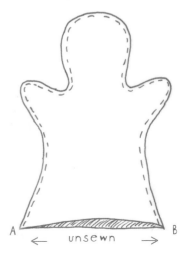

4 Turn the body right side out. Sew the beads for the eyes to the face, making sure to only go through the front layer of the body fabric. Use craft glue to attach pink felt circles for the cheeks, the plastic half-moon pieces for a mouth, and the shell for a nose. Cut twine pieces about 1/4 to 1/2 inch long for eyebrows. Apply craft glue and place them above the eyes. Allow glue to dry.

5 To make the hair, cut about three pieces of twine that are 16 inches long. You can cut more or less depending on how thick you would like the hair. The twine I used was made of three strands twisted together so I unraveled the pieces. Knot the three twine strands in the center. Place the center knot on top of the head and hand sew three to four times through the knot to attach the hair to the puppet.

6 Take the shoelace and cut two pieces about 3 inches long. Tie each shoelace around one side of the hair to make pigtails. Place a dot of craft glue on each end of the shoelace so it does not fray. Allow the glue to dry before you continue.

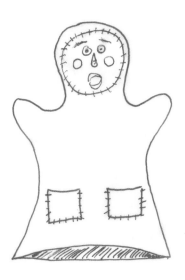

7 Preheat your hot glue gun. Place one burlap square on your work surface and stand the thread spool on top in the center of the square. Use a pencil to trace around the top of the spool. Cut out the center circle and set both pieces aside for now. Lay the uncut burlap square on your work surface. (You may need to place something under it to protect the work surface from the hot glue.) Apply a small amount of hot glue to the bottom of the spool and press it down in the center of the uncut square of burlap. This will form the bottom and brim of the hat. Place a few drops of glue on the brim. Push the top of the spool through the hole of the cut burlap just until it goes down over the edges of the spool. Apply hot glue around the spool and wrap the burlap rectangle around the spool to cover it. Trim any excess burlap if needed. Apply hot glue to the top of the spool and cover it with the cut-out circle of burlap.

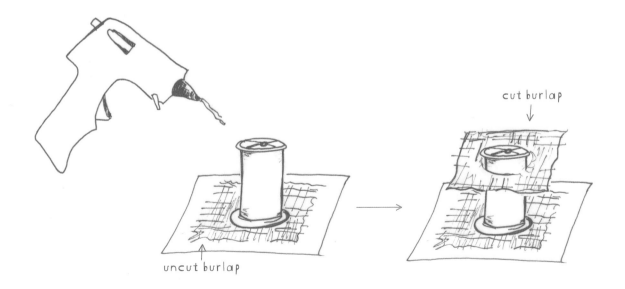

uncut burlap

cut burlap

8 Wrap ribbon around the hat and use craft or hot glue to attach the ends to the burlap on the back side of the hat.

9 Apply hot glue to the back of the piece of junk metal and attach it to the hat.

10 Place a dot of hot glue at the front corners underneath the hat brim and press along the hair to hold the hat in place.

BANJO INSTRUCTIONS

1 To make your wooden spoon banjo, take banjo shape A and glue it to the base of the spoon. Cut four pieces of black thread 9 inches long. Knot your thread at one end and bring it through one of the points of the card stock shape B to make the strings. Repeat with the remaining thread.

2 Apply hot glue on the back of the banjo shape B and press down on the banjo shape A. Bring the loose thread and needle through each of the points on shape D. Pull the thread taut and knot it at the back. Trim excess thread. Then apply hot glue on the back of the banjo shape C and place it 1/2 inch above shape B. Apply glue on banjo shape D and press down onto the end of the handle.

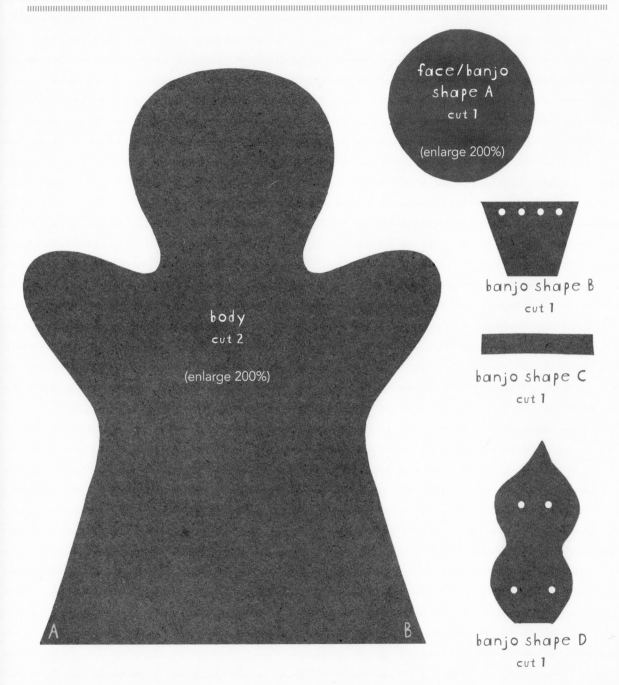

face/banjo
shape A
cut 1

(enlarge 200%)

banjo shape B
cut 1

banjo shape C
cut 1

body
cut 2

(enlarge 200%)

A

B

banjo shape D

cut 1

BETTY
THE ELEPHANT

LEVEL 2

Betty is known as the jokester in her family, always up to some shenanigan. One moment she flaps her powerful ears until the wind knocks you over and the next she slyly taps your shoulder with her trunk and then pretends she didn't do it.

Betty loves when guests come over for dinner, especially when they bring peanuts. Be sure to keep your eyes on your own plate—she may try to snatch an extra bite. Watch out after dessert: Betty is an adept tickle torturer, using her trunk to force you into a fit of chuckles.

MATERIALS

REUSED AND RECYCLED
2 gray leg warmers (the same or mismatched)

OTHER FABRIC
2 sheets of gray felt

EMBELLISHMENTS
2 black round dome shank buttons

small foam packing sponge or dish sponge

CONSTRUCTION MATERIALS AND TOOLS

ruler

fabric scissors

fabric marker or chalk

pins

sewing machine (optional)

sewing needle

thread to match the legwarmers

embroidery floss

embroidery needle

9

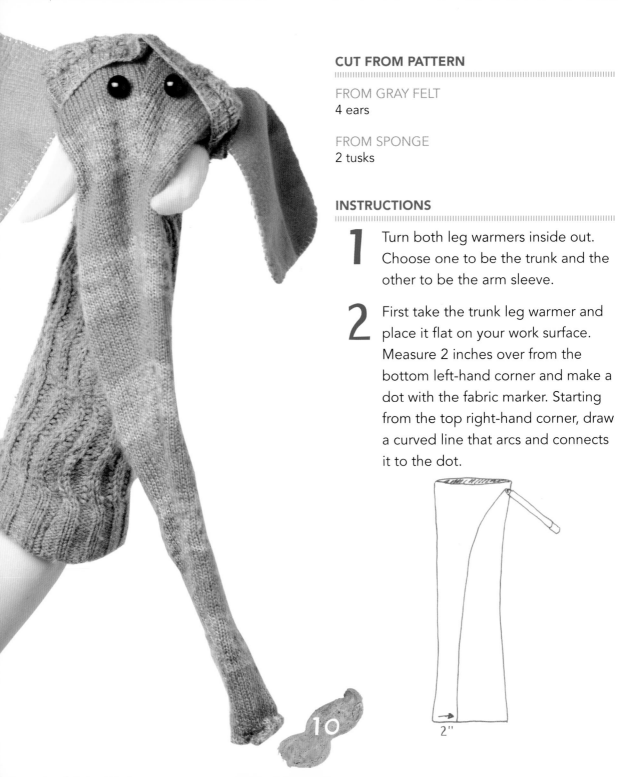

CUT FROM PATTERN

FROM GRAY FELT
4 ears

FROM SPONGE
2 tusks

INSTRUCTIONS

1 Turn both leg warmers inside out. Choose one to be the trunk and the other to be the arm sleeve.

2 First take the trunk leg warmer and place it flat on your work surface. Measure 2 inches over from the bottom left-hand corner and make a dot with the fabric marker. Starting from the top right-hand corner, draw a curved line that arcs and connects it to the dot.

2"

3 Place pins to either side of the line and machine sew or hand sew a backstitch or running stitch along the line. Trim the excess fabric so that it's 1/4 inch past the seam. Set the trunk aside for now.

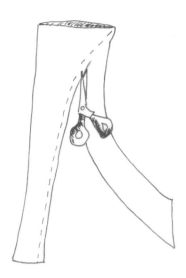

4 Fold the arm sleeve over to make a 2-inch cuff. Fold the wider side opening of the trunk over to make a 1/2-inch cuff. Place the arm sleeve and trunk cuffs together and pin them in place. Hand sew a whip stitch all the way around to attach the pieces at the edges.

5 Pin two ear shapes together and sew a blanket stitch with three strands of embroidery floss along the edges. Leave side X of the ears unsewn. Repeat with the other two ear shapes.

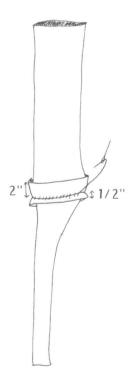

2"   1/2"

6 Align both ears to the side of the arm sleeve leg warmer. The ears should be about 5 inches apart, measuring along the top of the head. Pin the front and back sides of the ears to the leg warmer, pulling the front side 1/4 inch forward to leave a gap between the front and back sides of the ears so they will stand out away from the head. Hand sew along the edges of the ears to attach them to the arm sleeve cuff edges.

7 Align the button eyes about 1 1/2 inches apart and about 1 inch down from the top of the trunk. Use thread to sew them to the trunk.

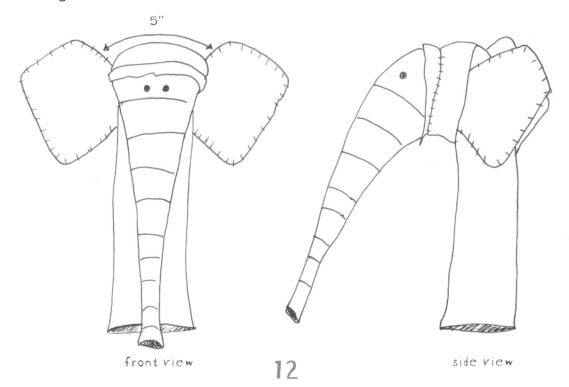

front view

side view

8 Use fabric scissors to shape the tusks. Round the edges by trimming the sponge with fabric scissors. (Note: Cutting foam may dull the blades.) Place the tusks so they are between the cuffs. Pinch the sides of arm sleeve and trunk cuff together and pin them on either side of the tusks. Begin hand sewing a few stitches to connect the two cuffs on one side of the tusk and then sew into and through the foam tusk and back out two times. Then sew a few stitches on the other side of the cuff to secure the tusks.

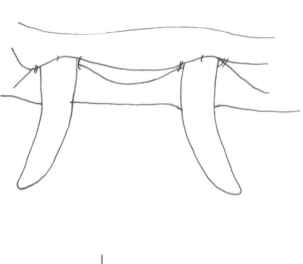

9 Pinch the end opening of the trunk together and hand sew a few stitches in the center, leaving the outside edges unsewn to create two nostrils.

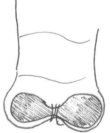

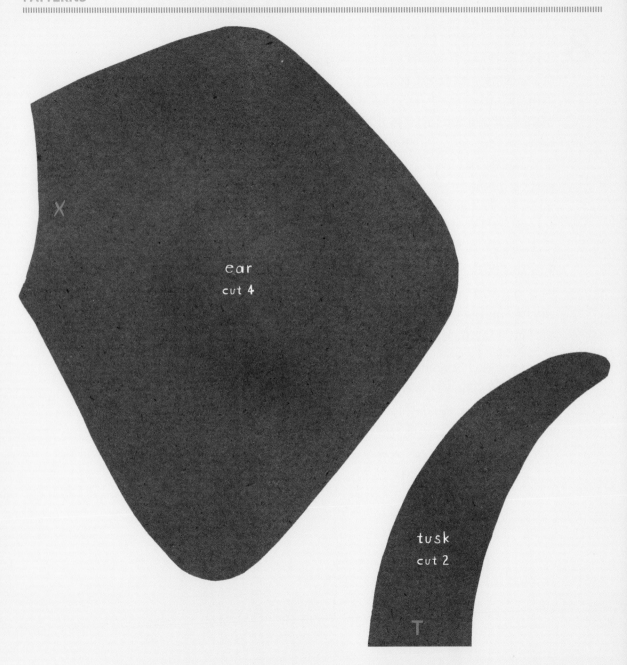

ear
cut 4

X

tusk
cut 2

T

FEILONG
THE DRAGON

LEVEL 3

Feilong is a spiritual Chinese dragon that appears to be part lizard, bull, and tiger. He lives up in the clouds and mist, controlling the rainfall. If he is pleased he will allow plentiful rain for the harvest. If he is angry he will send storm clouds to flood the land. If you catch a glimpse of the dragon flying above, it is a sign your life will be prosperous.

MATERIALS

REUSED AND RECYCLED

1 yellow rubber kitchen glove

1 red leg warmer, sweater sleeve, shirt sleeve, or scarf (if you use a scarf you will need to fold it in half lengthwise and sew a seam)

1 scrap of white felt

1 scrap of red felt

1 scrap of black felt, about 2 x 3 inches

2 wire hangers

OTHER FABRIC

2 sheets of yellow felt

EMBELLISHMENTS

1 (14-inch) shoelace, cord, or ribbon

2 bottle caps

1 foam packing sponge or dish sponge

braided cord from a shopping/gift bag

CONSTRUCTION MATERIALS AND TOOLS

ruler

fabric scissors

stuffing

sewing needle

yellow thread

red thread

black thread

pins

hot glue gun

wire cutters

pliers

masking tape

craft glue

CUT FROM PATTERN

FROM YELLOW FELT
8 feet

1 tongue

2 eyebrows

2 back shapes

FROM RED FELT
2 ears

FROM FOAM/SPONGE
2 horns

4 triangular teeth

CUT FREEHAND

FROM WHITE FELT
2 small pupils

FROM BLACK FELT
2 circles that will fit on the inside of the bottle caps

2 rectangles, about 2 x 2 1/2 inches

FROM RED FELT
2 rectangles 1/2 x 1 inch

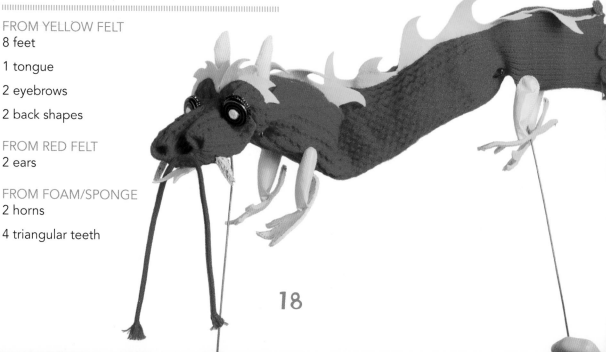

18

INSTRUCTIONS

1 Cut the ends off of four fingers of the rubber glove so the cut-off ends are all even and about 2 1/2 inches long. These will be the legs. Place a pinch of stuffing in each leg so there is just enough to give it a little shape. Use yellow thread to hand sew a whip stitch around the edge of each opening to close it up.

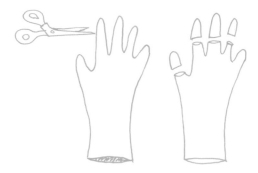

2 Pin two feet shapes together, matching edges. Use red thread to sew a running stitch around the edges of the feet about 1/4 inch from the edges. Repeat with the remaining feet so you have two left and two right feet.

3 Place the sewn side of one glove against one foot and sew a few stitches at each X to attach them. Repeat with the remaining feet and legs, and set them aside.

4 Place the leg warmer flat on your work surface, right side out. This will become the dragon's body. If there is a smaller end, use it for the head side. For the head, hand sew a whip stitch about 1 1/4 inch long across the middle of the open end, leaving the sides open to form the nostrils.

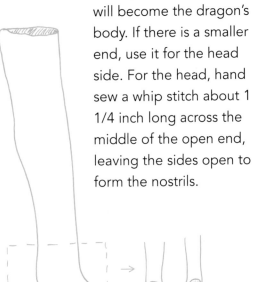

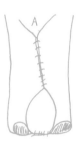

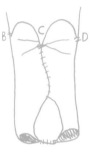

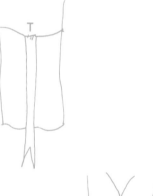

5 Pinch together the fabric in the middle, between the nostrils, to scrunch up the face a little. Pin it in place. Use red thread to whip stitch the middle section together starting about 1 1/2 inches from the end and sew 1 1/2 inches closed, stopping at point A.

6 About 3 1/2 inches from the end of the nose, pinch the leg warmer fabric forward to shape the head. Use red thread to tack it down with a few stitches at points B, C, and D.

7 Use yellow thread to sew the tongue to the underside of the nostrils in the fold of the leg warmer at point T. If you don't want the tongue to hang you can tack it down at the edge of the mouth.

8 Preheat your hot glue gun while you make the dragon's whiskers. Place the middle of the shoelace in between the nostrils and attach with a few stitches of red thread at point E.

9 Use a dot of hot glue to apply one white pupil to the inside of each bottle cap. Then apply a dot of hot glue on each pupil and attach a black circle to each. Finally, place a dot of hot glue on the back of each bottle cap and attach them to the head where the eyes should go.

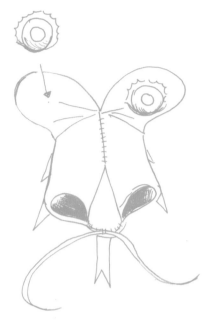

10 Place a drop of hot glue on the flat side of each tooth and attach them along the underside of the mouth.

11 Align the eyebrows above the eyes and use yellow thread to whip stitch them to the leg warmer.

12 Use scissors to trim the foam horns and round the edges. Place a dot of hot glue at the flat end of each horn and stick one behind each eyebrow, about 1/2 to 3/4 inch back.

13 Use red thread to sew the ears to the side of the head.

14 Center the flat side of a back shape along the leg warmer and pin in place. Place the second back shape right next to the first and pin it, too. You may need to trim excess felt off of an end, depending on how long the body of your dragon is. Sew a whip stitch all the way along the edge to connect the felt to the body.

15 Place a small amount of stuffing inside the body so there is just enough to give it shape.

16 To make rods, use wire cutters to cut the hangers so you have two pieces that are 15 inches long. Use pliers to gently bend a loop at each end. Then bend 1 inch of the wire at a 90 degree angle. Wrap the opposite end of the wire with masking tape and wrap and glue the black felt rectangle to cover it.

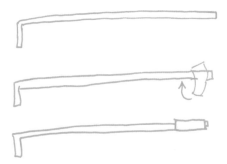

17 Place the first rod 1 to 2 inches in front of the legs on the underside of the belly. Place a rectangle of red felt around the bent part of the wire and wrap around. Hand sew felt with red thread to the underside of the body. Repeat with the second rod, attaching slightly in front of the back legs.

PATTERNS

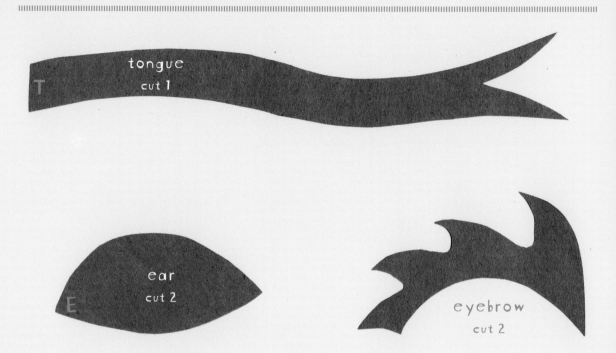

tongue
cut 1

T

ear
cut 2

E

eyebrow
cut 2

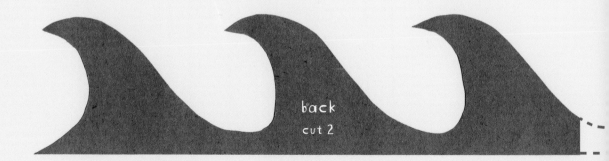

back
cut 2

horn
cut 2

foot
cut 8

tooth
cut 4

Cut out the two back pattern pieces and attach them at the center before tracing the complete piece on your felt.

DOTTIE THE CLOWN

LEVEL 2

Dottie is a jittery and klutzy clown. Her humor comes from her nervousness. She has unusual acts such as juggling eggs, riding a unicycle , and making unrecognizable balloon animals. A show is never complete without an audience member having a head covered in egg yolk or Dottie falling flat on her face. In the end Dottie always receives applause. She will usually offer a pie to be thrown at her face as a farewell.

MATERIALS

REUSED AND RECYCLED
1 dish or tea towel

1 scrap of light blue felt

OTHER FABRIC
1 sheet of yellow felt

EMBELLISHMENTS
multi-colored yarn

1 large red pom pom

2 small metal washers

1 blue plastic key cover

9 inches of light green ribbon

vegetable netting

2 small fake flowers

CONSTRUCTION MATERIALS AND TOOLS

ruler

fabric scissors

pins

sewing machine (optional)

sewing needle

yellow thread

stuffing

craft glue

CUT FROM PATTERN

FROM TEA TOWEL

2 body shapes

2 hat shapes

FROM YELLOW FELT

1 face

2 ears

FROM LIGHT BLUE FELT

1 pocket

INSTRUCTIONS

1 Place one body shape right side up on your work surface. Center the felt face on the head, pin it in place, and machine or hand sew a backstitch or running stitch around the edges of the face with yellow thread.

2 Place the ears on the head, matching points E to E and lining up the inside edges of the ears with the edges of the head. The outer lobes of the ears should be pointing in toward the body. The ears can be slightly angled. Place the body shapes right sides together, matching edges, and pin them. Starting at point A, hand sew or machine sew about 1/4 inch from the edges around the body to point B, leaving the hand opening unsewn.

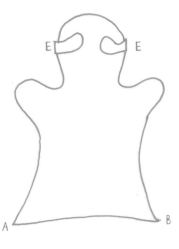

3 Turn the body right side out and set it aside.

4 Place both hat shapes right side up on your work surface. Fold each along the dotted line from point X to point X to the wrong side and pin. Machine sew to make a seam. Repeat with the other hat piece.

5 Place one hat shape right side up on your work surface. Place the second hat shape right side down on top and pin together. Hand or machine sew along diagonals from point X to point Y, leaving side (X–X) open. Turn right sides out.

6 Cut four strands of yarn that are 2 to 4 inches long. Use one strand to tie a double knot at the center of the other three strands. Sew two to three stitches through the yarn knot at Y. Place a pinch of stuffing inside the hat and set it aside.

7 Place the pom pom nose on the face and sew three stitches to attach it. Then use a small amount of craft glue on the back of the washers and glue them in place for the eyes. Apply a small amount of glue to the back of the key cover and attach it for the mouth. Allow the glue to dry before you continue.

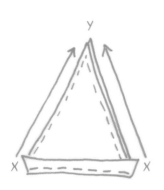

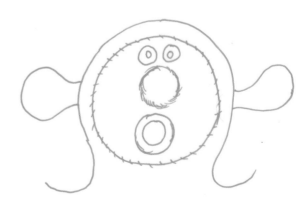

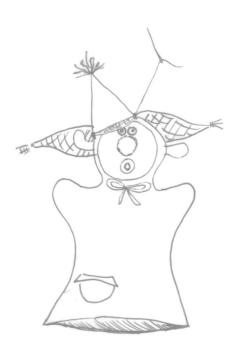

8 Place the pocket on the front of the body. Fold the top down in front of the pocket and pin the pocket in place. Hand sew around the outside edge of the pocket, leaving the top edge unsewn.

9 Tie a bow with the ribbon. Hand sew a few stitches through the knot to attach the bow below the face.

10 For the hair, find the center of the vegetable netting and pinch it together. Wrap thread around it a few times and knot the thread. Place the center of the netting at the center of the top of the head and sew a few stitches through the netting at the knot to attach it. Arrange the hat so it is askew at one side of the head, making sure the knot in the netting is hidden under the edge of the hat. Pin the hat in place and sew two to three stitches at each corner of the hat to attach it to the head.

11 Place the flowers inside the pocket.

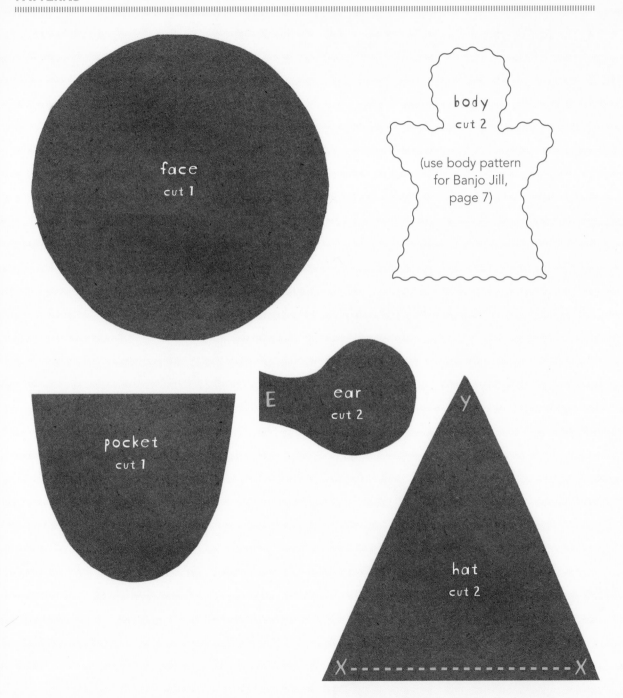

face
cut 1

body
cut 2

(use body pattern
for Banjo Jill,
page 7)

pocket
cut 1

E   ear
cut 2

y

hat
cut 2

X - - - - - - - - - - - - - - - X

CRAZY CAT

LEVEL 1

This freaky feline's whiskers are messy for a reason. He's berserk! Sure he looks like a cat, but he does not act like one. Poor Crazy Cat has a bad memory and gets all mixed up. No meows are heard from this fella. Some days he barks, other days he chirps, and occasionally he may moo.

MATERIALS

REUSED AND RECYCLED

1 leg warmer, sweater sleeve, or scarf (if you use a scarf, you will need to fold in half lengthwise and sew a seam down the side)

1 scrap of brown felt

OTHER FABRIC

1 sheet of navy blue felt

EMBELLISHMENTS

tape from an old cassette tape, or 3 shoelaces, or some yarn

2 buttons that are different colors and sizes

1 pipe cleaner

CONSTRUCTION MATERIALS AND TOOLS

ruler

fabric scissors

pins

sewing needle

brown thread

navy blue thread

craft glue

CUT FROM PATTERN

FROM NAVY BLUE FELT

4 ear shapes

1 tail shape

FROM BROWN FELT

1 nose

2 eye pupils (Use a coin for your pattern shape. Trace two but trim one pupil so it is smaller than the other.)

32

INSTRUCTIONS

1 Place the leg warmer, sweater sleeve, or scarf on your work surface. This will be the body. If there is a smaller end, use that for the head. For example, I used the 9-inch diameter opening for the head and the 10 1/2-inch diameter opening for the arm sleeve.

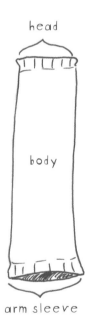

2 Fold the top down about 4 inches. Pinch the fabric at the center bottom of the head and fold the opening of the leg warmer or sweater sleeve in to make a U-shape and pin it together. Sew a whip stitch down 1 1/2 inches. Sew three to four stitches to tack down the nose opening to the head at point A, making sure you only sew through the front layer of the leg warmer or sweater sleeve.

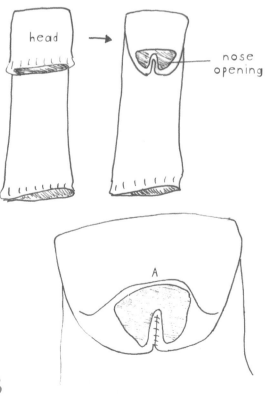

3 Use the cassette tape, shoelaces, or yarn to make the whiskers. Cut three 7- to 10-inch strands and double knot them together in the center. Sew a few stitches through the whisker knot to the nose area at point B, making sure you only sew through one layer of the leg warmer or sweater sleeve.

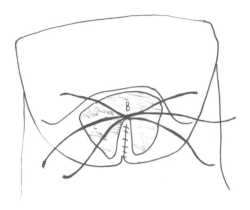

4 Place the nose shape on top of the nose opening and whiskers, adjust the whiskers, and pin it in place. If the nose looks too small for the face, you may need to pinch in the opening a little more and repin it before sewing on the nose shape. You can also cut a larger nose shape. Using the brown thread, whip stitch around the edges of the nose to attach it along the opening, making sure to sew around the whiskers and you only go through one layer of the leg warmer or sleeve.

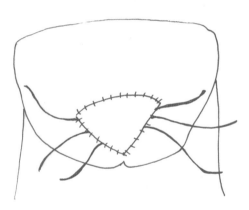

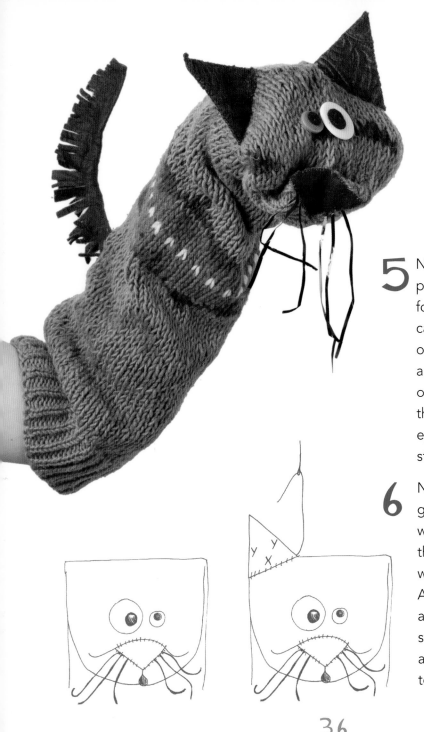

5 Next comes the look of the puppet's eyes and the pupil focus. For example, I made this cat cross-eyed. Align the pupils on buttons where you like them and either glue them in place or sew a few stitches through the buttonholes. Then place the eyes on the head and sew a few stitches to secure them.

6 Now pin two ear shapes together, matching edges, and whip stitch along sides Y, using the navy blue thread. Repeat with the other two ear shapes. Align the ears on the head at an angle and pin in place. Whip stitch along side X on the front and back side to attach the ears to the head.

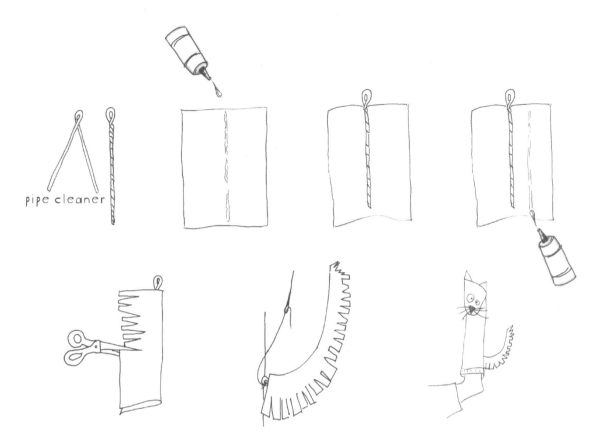

pipe cleaner

7 To make the tail, fold the pipe cleaner in half and twist, leaving a small loop at one end. Apply craft glue lengthwise down the center of the rectangle of navy blue felt. Place the pipe cleaner so that the loop end sticks out beyond the edge of the felt. Apply a small amount of glue down one side of the felt, fold it in half, and press together. Allow it to dry before you continue.

8 Use fabric scissors to cut the tail horizontally or diagonally toward the pipe cleaner to give it a frayed look. Decide how far down you want the tail placed along the center back of the arm sleeve. Hand sew through the loop end of the pipe cleaner and into the leg warmer to attach the tail. Bend the tail to curve it.

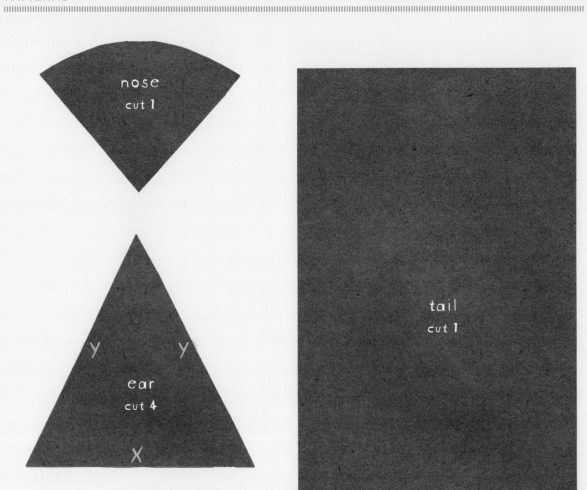

nose
cut 1

y   y

ear
cut 4

X

tail
cut 1

FROGGY AND HIS FLY FEAST

LEVEL 2

Buford was a champion jumper in his younger days, but now he spends most of his time in the muggy swamp leisurely leaping from log to leaf. At dusk, when the flies and mosquitoes are out, Buford knows supper will be a quick catch. He stays up late into the night with other swamp frogs, gossiping about the freshest flies and the longest leaps. Ribbit!

MATERIALS

REUSED AND RECYCLED
1 green bandana (preferably at least 20 x 20 inches)

cardboard from a standard cereal box

2 egg cups cut from a cardboard egg carton

1 scrap of yellow felt

OTHER FABRIC
1 sheet of black felt

1 sheet of green felt

EMBELLISHMENTS
1 red fabric handle from a shopping bag with a bendable wire

2 small buttons

1 pom pom

2 alphabet beads

1 cotton swab

fishing line

1 popsicle stick

39

CONSTRUCTION MATERIALS AND TOOLS

ruler

fabric scissors

sewing machine (optional)

sewing needle

thread

pins

fabric marker

craft glue

paint brush

hot glue gun

light green paint

CUT FROM PATTERN

FROM BLACK FELT

1 mouth

1 shape A

1 fly eyebrow

FROM CARDBOARD

1 mouth

FROM YELLOW FELT

2 wing shapes

CUT FREEHAND

FROM GREEN FELT

1 rectangle, 1 3/4 x 11 inches

INSTRUCTIONS

1 Start with placing the bandana on your work space and cutting it into a 20 x 20-inch square. If you use a smaller size bandana reduce the size of the mouth pattern accordingly.

2 Next make the arm sleeve by folding the bandana in half with the right sides together and pin in place. Machine or hand sew a backstitch or running stitch down the side 1/4 inch from the edges.

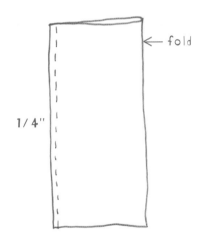

3 Next, sew a 1/4-inch seam 5 inches from the vertical seam. Measure 6 inches down from the top from the folded side and use a fabric pen to make a mark. Trace a line from the end of the top seam to the mark and cut. Set the bandana aside.

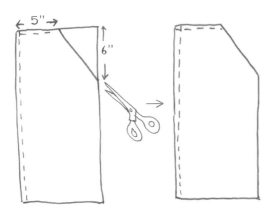

4 Cut a small hole in the center of the felt mouth for the tongue. Bend the fabric shopping bag handle 1 inch and curl the rest of the tongue. Stick the straight, bent section through the front of the mouth shape to the back.

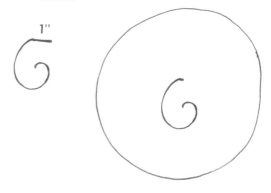

5 Glue shape A over the back section of the tongue to attach it to the felt.

42

6 Lay the bandana flat so the side seam is centered on the back facing the work surface and the hole is facing up. Align the mouth so it overlaps the top and bottom seam by 1/4 to 1/2 inch. Sew a whip stitch around the mouth to attach it to the bandana. Fold down the nose tip from points N to N. Sew three stitches on either side to hold in place. This will form the frog's nostrils.

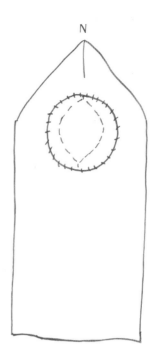

7 Turn the bandana wrong side out. Fold the cardboard in half to make an inside mouthpiece. Apply glue on the inside of the folded cardboard and press it onto the felt so the fold is horizontal. Once dry you can turn the bandana right side out again.

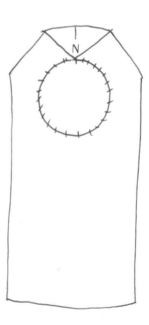

8 Paint the outsides of the egg cups with light green paint and allow them to dry completely. Glue a button to the center bottom of each egg cup.

9 Preheat your hot glue gun. Align the egg carton eyes on the head by measuring 3 inches up from the nose tip at N to point X and space the eyes 2 1/4 inches apart. Use a small amount of hot glue to hold the eyes down. Place the green felt rectangle on the head, aligning it so it covers the tops of the eyes and overhangs them a little. Hand sew the felt to the head.

front view

FLY FEAST

1 Hand sew both wings into either side of the pom pom.

2 Glue alphabet bead eyes to the pom pom. Place the eyebrow shape above the beads as a unibrow and glue it in place.

3 Cut off the head of the cotton swab and glue it to the pom pom with craft glue.

4 Sew fishing line into the top of the pom pom. Tie fishing line to the popsicle stick so the fly can hang above and the frog can catch it.

top view

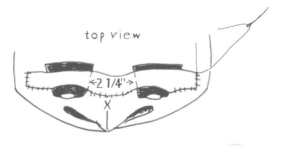

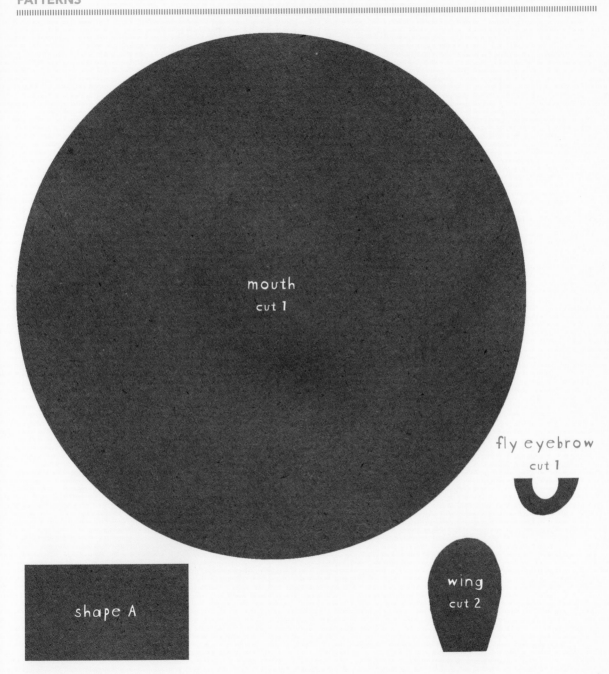

mouth
cut 1

fly eyebrow
cut 1

shape A

wing
cut 2

ICE CREAM MAN

LEVEL 1

Jeff the Ice Cream Man sells homemade ice cream from his shop all summer long. Although he has simple flavors, such as chocolate, vanilla, and strawberry, he has created quite a stir with his experimental ice cream concoctions. Bored with the standard ice cream menu, he has created flavors such as tomato-popcorn, raisin and cheddar, asparagus, and spicy fried sardines. His customers haven't caught on as much as he hoped, but Jeff believes his new mystery flavor will be a success. Any guesses?

MATERIALS

REUSED AND RECYCLED
1 polka dot knee-high sock

1 scrap of light brown felt

1 scrap of dark brown felt

1 scrap of black felt

OTHER FABRIC
1 sheet of white or ivory felt

46

EMBELLISHMENTS
1 large pom pom

1 mini red pom pom

3 small black buttons

2 large googly eyes

CONSTRUCTION MATERIALS AND TOOLS
ruler

fabric scissors

sewing needle

light brown thread

black thread

white thread

pins

craft glue

pinch of stuffing

fabric marker

CUT FROM PATTERN

FROM WHITE FELT
2 hat shapes

1 brim

FROM LIGHT BROWN FELT
2 cone shapes

FROM BLACK FELT
1 bow tie

CUT FREEHAND

FROM WHITE FELT
1 square, 1 inch x 1 inch

FROM DARK BROWN FELT
7 to 9 small diamond shapes

INSTRUCTIONS

1 Start by making the ice cream cone. Place the two cone shapes together, matching edges, pin them, and sew a whip stitch down the sides with light brown thread. Leave the top unsewn.

2 Place a small amount of craft glue on each felt diamond shape and arrange them on the front of the cone. Allow the glue to dry before continuing.

3 Place a pinch of stuffing into the cone to give it some shape. Sew through the corners of the cone and into the large pom pom to attach it to the cone. Place the mini red pom pom on top of larger pom pom and sew a few stitches to attach it. Set the ice cream cone aside.

4 Cut the sheet of white felt in half crosswise. Use one piece to make the shirt. Lay it crosswise on your work surface and fold the top back 1/2 inch toward the work surface to make the collar. Pin it in place. Place the sock on the folded felt, heel side up. The top of the shirt collar should rest just below your wrist when your hand is in the puppet. Adjust the sock accordingly, then wrap the shirt around the sock so the open side will be in the back (heel side) and pin the edges together at the top. Hand sew about 1/2 inch down the back of the shirt to close the side. Then hand sew a few stitches to tack the shirt to the sock in front.

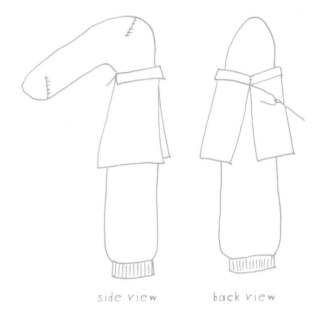

side view   back view

49

5 Cut a triangle out in the center of the collar for the bow tie. Twist the bow tie once and hand stitch with black thread through the middle to attach it to the shirt. Arrange the buttons down the middle of the shirt, mark with a fabric marker, and then sew the buttons to the shirt. Place the square felt shape as a pocket on the chest and hand sew with white thread along the side and bottom edges, leaving the top unsewn. Then place the ice cream cone on the shirt and sew a few hidden stitches from behind it to attach it.

6 Fold the top of the sock over as if a hand were in it. Align the googly eyes and attach them with a small amount of craft glue. Allow them to dry before you continue.

7 Place the two hat shapes together, matching edges, and sew along the top, leaving side H (the bottom) open. Wrap the brim around the bottom of the hat, matching edges. Hand sew with white thread along the bottom to attach the pieces. Place the hat on the head so the open section of brim is in front, and sew a few stitches to hold the hat in place.

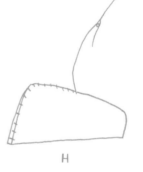

H

PATTERNS

bow tie
cut 1

hat
cut 2

H

cone
cut 2

brim
cut 1

H

H

KANGAROO CARLY AND ZACK

LEVEL 2

The hopping duo of Kangaroo Carly and Zack were once unknown marsupials in the arid outback of Australia. Now they are famous for their jumping abilities. Together they compete in jumping events in the Outback Olympics. In the past they have placed in the top three. This year they have been madly training, taking just short breaks. Rumor is that they will easily take first place this year.

MATERIALS

REUSED AND RECYCLED
1 convertible mitten or glove*

OTHER FABRIC
1 sheet of turquoise felt

EMBELLISHMENTS
2 metallic beads

2 snaps

2 plastic half-moon shapes (optional)

2 white seed beads

*If you use a regular glove cut out 1 pocket shape from the felt or another fabric.

CONSTRUCTION MATERIALS AND TOOLS

ruler

fabric scissors

sewing needle

turquoise thread

black thread

white thread

pins

craft glue

stuffing

fabric marker

CUT FROM PATTERN

FROM FELT

4 arm shapes

4 leg shapes

2 large head shapes

2 large ears

2 small head shapes

1 triangle shape

2 small ear shapes

INSTRUCTIONS

1 Place two arm shapes together, matching edges, and whip stitch around the edges using the turquoise thread, leaving side X unsewn for a pinky and pointer finger opening. Repeat with the other two arm shapes, and set the arms aside.

2 Place the two leg shapes together, matching edges, and whip stitch around the edges, leaving side Y unsewn. Repeat with the other two leg shapes, and set the legs aside.

3 Place the two large head shapes together, matching edges, and whip stitch around the edges, leaving side A unsewn for a middle and ring finger opening.

4 Take the two large ear shapes and sew a whip stitch along the edge from points C to D. Then place each ear to large head, D to D, and sew a few stitches to attach at D.

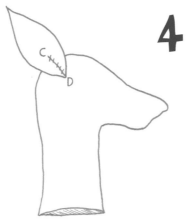

5 Arrange the metal beads on the large head for eyes and sew a few stitches to attach them. Apply a small amount of craft glue to the backs of the plastic parts and place them for eyebrows if desired. Allow the glue to dry.

6 Place a snap on the nose at point N and use black thread to sew two stitches on either side to attach it. Use a pinch of stuffing to fill the head and set it aside.

7 Place the two small head shapes together, matching edges, and pin them. Align the triangle shape on the head, matching points T to T. Sew a whip stitch around the edges to attach all the shapes together, leaving side B unsewn for a thumb opening.

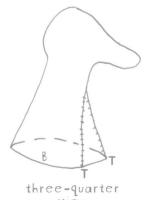

three-quarter
view

front view

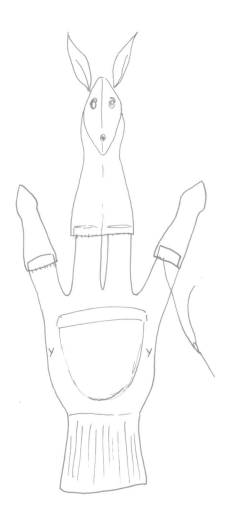

8 Take the small ears and stitch each ear on either side of the small head at point E. Attach the small white beads with a few stitches of white thread to form the eyes.

9 Place a snap on the nose at point N and sew two stitches with black thread on either side to attach it. Use a pinch of stuffing to fill the head and set it aside.

10 Fit the glove over your hand. Place the arms over the pinky and pointer fingers of the glove, sliding them down until they feel fitted but not too tight. Make a mark for the placement. Remove the glove from your hand. Whip stitch around the bottom edges of the arms to attach them to the glove. Repeat this step to attach the large head over the middle and ring fingers together.

11 Cut a small hole through the back of the pocket and the point behind the pocket where it meets the glove to allow your thumb to go through. Fit the glove over your hand, then fit the small head over your thumb. Center the head and mark the placement to the inside of the pocket. Whip stitch with turquoise thread around the edge of the head to attach it to the glove.

If you do not use a convertible glove, cut a small hole through the front of the glove for the thumb. Then place the pocket shape on and sew around the edges of the pocket to attach it to the glove. Then continue to sew the small head.

12 Pin the legs to the glove, matching points Y to Y, and sew with turquoise thread a whip stitch along the sides to attach the legs to the glove.

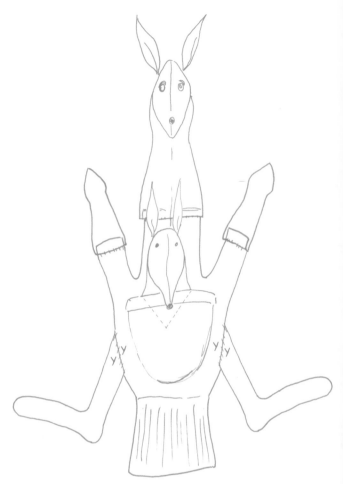

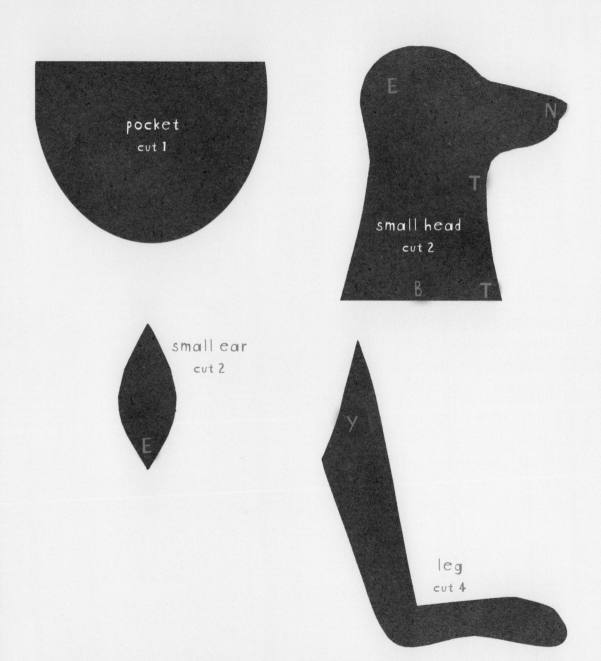

pocket
cut 1

small head
cut 2

E

N

T

B   T

small ear
cut 2

E

y

leg
cut 4

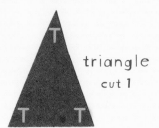

triangle
cut 1

arm
cut 4

X

D

N

large head
cut 2

A

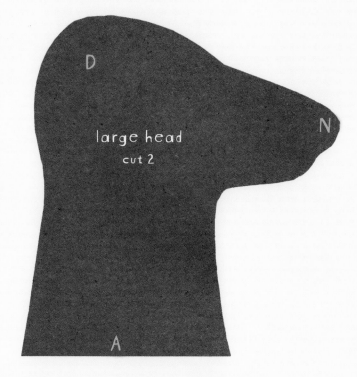

large ear
cut 2

C

D

PUNK ROCKER

LEVEL 1

Skid is the drummer in the punk rock band Mourning Breath. He is currently working on the band's new album, *Chew This*. Skid is known as the philosophical band member and has written hits such as "Green Cheeseburger Woes" and "Where's my shoe? Where's my house key?" He is currently working on the song "Come back, dog!" in honor of his beloved pit bull named Sid. Skid's bandmates are afraid to tell him that Sid ran off with the neighborhood poodle, Nancy.

MATERIALS

REUSED AND RECYCLED

1 scrap of faux fur, approximately 3/4 inch wide x 4 inches long

1 scrap of black fabric from an old t-shirt, or other black cotton material

1 scrap of white cotton from a rag, holey t-shirt, or undershirt

scraps of cotton print for patches (I cut out a piece from a pirate print bandana)

1 scrap of fabric such as reptile pleather or vinyl, about 2 inches x 1/2 inch

OTHER FABRIC

1 sheet of blue felt

EMBELLISHMENTS

buttons and metal pieces for jewelry

2 foam ear bud covers for headphones

2 small colorful beads

hook from a hook-and-eye fastener

assorted buttons/pins with images on them

10 safety pins

CONSTRUCTION MATERIALS AND TOOLS

ruler

fabric scissors

craft glue

pins

sewing machine (optional)

sewing needle

blue thread

black thread

red thread (or another bright color)

CUT FROM PATTERN

FROM BLACK COTTON
2 body shapes

FROM WHITE COTTON
2 shirt shapes

FROM BLUE FELT
1 face

2 ears

INSTRUCTIONS

1 Start with faux fur fabric. Mix a small amount of craft glue with a few drops of water and use it to twist and shape the hair into a mohawk style. Set the hair aside to dry.

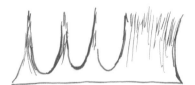

2 Place one body shape right side up on your work surface. Center the felt face on the head, pin it in place, and use blue thread to machine or hand sew a backstitch or whipstitch around the edges of the face. Place the ears on the head, matching points E to E, with the outer lobes of the ear pointing in toward the body, and pin them in place. The ears can be slightly angled. Place the body shapes right sides together, matching edges, and pin them. Starting at point A, use black thread to machine or hand sew a backstitch or running stitch about 1/4 inch from the edges around the body to point B, leaving the hand opening unsewn. Turn the body right side out.

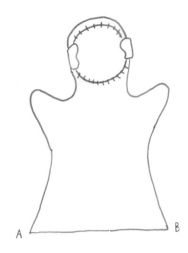

3 Hand sew buttons and metal pieces onto the ears for jewelry. To make the eyes, place the ear bud covers on the felt face and sew through the centers with black thread to attach them to the face. Place a drop of craft glue on the back of each colorful bead and attach it to the center of an ear bud cover. Allow the glue to dry before you continue.

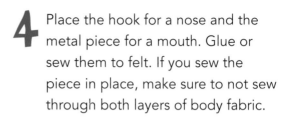

4 Place the hook for a nose and the metal piece for a mouth. Glue or sew them to felt. If you sew the piece in place, make sure to not sew through both layers of body fabric.

5 The cotton fabric I used for the shirt was already worn and holey. If you need more holes, cut small horizontal slits. Choose which side will be the front and which will be the back. Pin the patches in place and sew them on using a bright color of thread, such as red, making irregular cross-stitches or whip stitches. Pin on the buttons.

6 Place the back of the t-shirt right side down on your work surface. Then place the puppet body right side up on top. Next, place the front side of the t-shirt on top, with the right side facing up. Attach all of the pieces using four safety pins along the left side, four along the right side, and two on top.

7 To make a bracelet, fold the reptile pleather or vinyl fabric in half cross-wise and sew a whip stitch along the edges. Turn it so that the sewn edges are facing the inside of the loop. Place the bracelet on one of the puppet arms.

8 Center the mohawk on the face about 1/2 inch down from the top of the face and continuing over to the back of the body. Pin it in place and hand sew a whip stitch with blue thread along the edge or use craft glue to attach it to the head.

side view

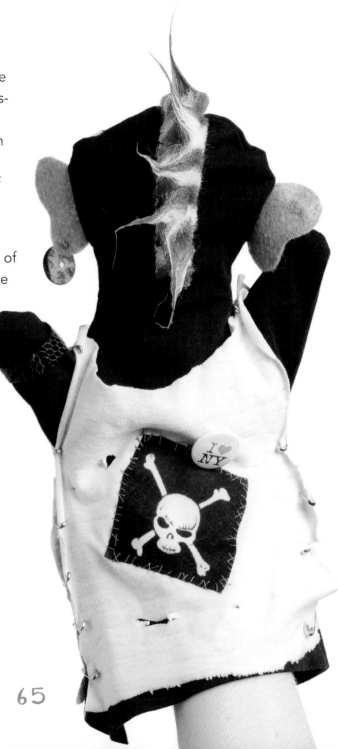

65

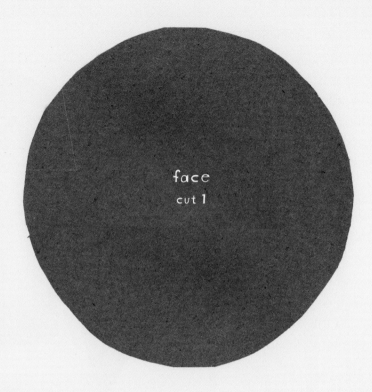

face

cut 1

ear

cut 2

E

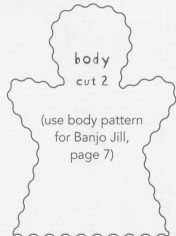

body

cut 2

(use body pattern
for Banjo Jill,
page 7)

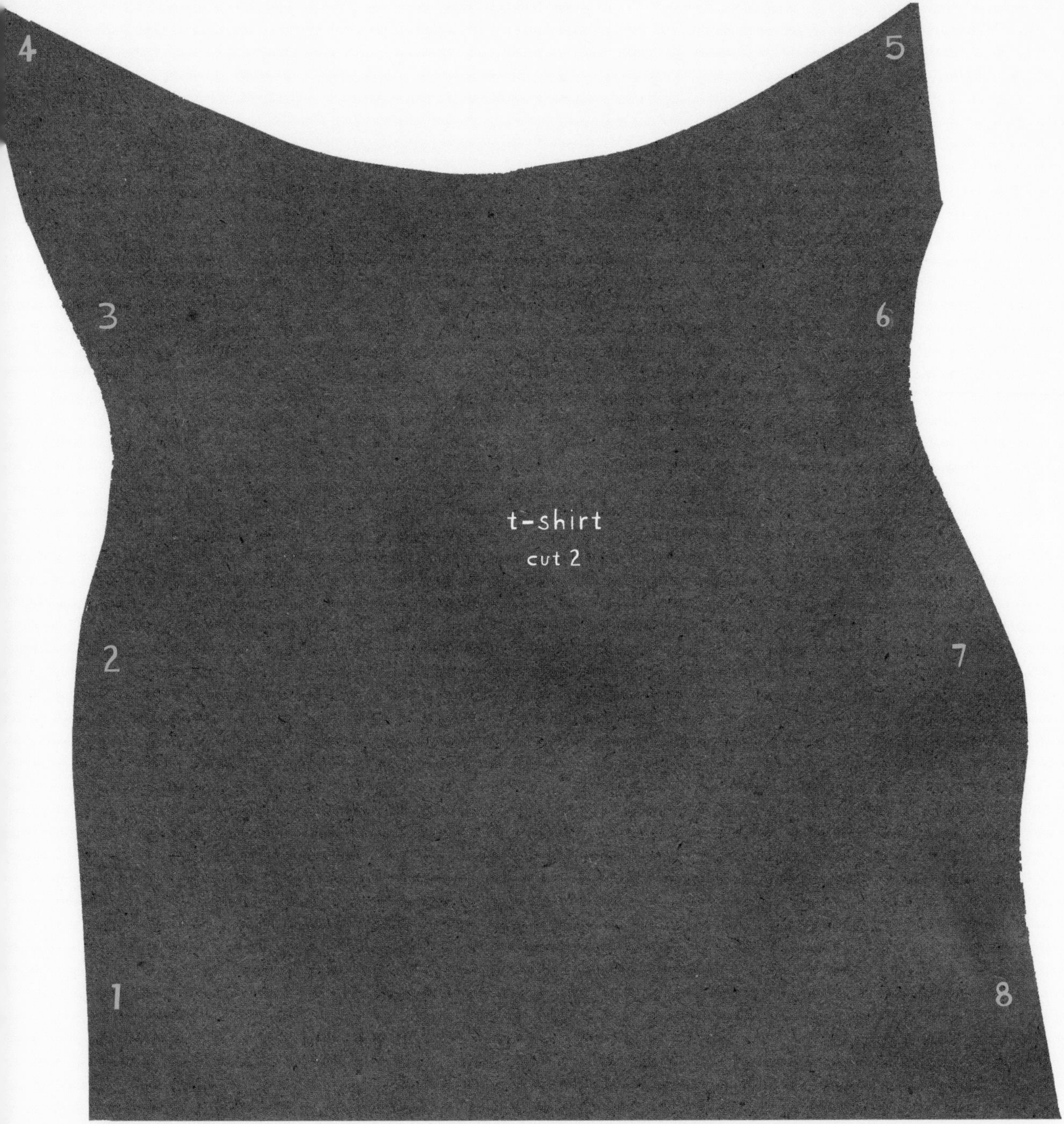

t-shirt

cut 2

4

5

3

6

2

7

1

8

ROSLYN RACCOON

LEVEL 1

Roslyn Raccoon used to only dine on fine berries and acorns. New neighbors moved in and her food tastes expanded. She has proclaimed herself a "nocturnal foodie," while other animals just call her a trash addict. When the night is quiet Roslyn heads out with her coon crew and pries open rubbish bins. Deep-dish meat pizza crusts, big stinky cheeses, mayonnaise sandwiches, and clotted curdled cream are a few of her favorite foods. She believes "a garbage can is a treasure trove of leftover delights."

MATERIALS

REUSED AND RECYCLED
1 black or salt-and-pepper colored mitten

1 scrap of blue felt

1 scrap of gray felt

OTHER FABRIC
1 sheet of black felt

1/2 sheet of white felt

EMBELLISHMENTS
1 toggle button

2 googly eyes

CONSTRUCTION MATERIALS AND TOOLS

ruler

fabric scissors

sewing needle

black thread

white thread

craft glue

fabric marker or chalk

CUT FROM PATTERN

FROM BLACK FELT
2 ears

1 eye mask

2 arms

FROM WHITE FELT

1 head

2 stripes

FROM GRAY FELT

2 hands

CUT FREEHAND

FROM BLUE FELT

2 small circles bigger than the googly eyes

INSTRUCTIONS

1 Place the eye mask shape on top of the head shape, matching points X to X. Hand sew a whip stitch with black thread along X–X.

2 Place the mitten flat on your work surface so the thumb is facing up and centered in the middle. The hand opening should be facing up and away from you, the tip toward you.

3 Place the head shape/eye mask on top of the mitten, aligning it along the curve of the mitten. Hand sew with white thread to attach the pieces along the edge.

70

4 Place the toggle button at point N for the nose. Sew four to five stitches through the button and the tip of the mitten to secure it in place.

5 Use a little craft glue to attach the googly eyes so they are centered on top of each piece of blue felt. Place the eyes on top of the eye mask and glue them in place. Set aside to dry.

6 Place one arm shape on your work surface. Take one hand and align side H to H. Fold the arm in half and sew a whip stitch with black thread along the edge C–D. When you sew over the hands you can switch to a backstitch and then back to a whip stitch if it is easier. Repeat with the remaining arm and hand.

7 Place the mitten on your hand and use a fabric marker or chalk to mark the areas along the sides where your thumb and pinky finger will need holes to work the raccoon's arms.

8 Now place the mitten on a work surface thumb side down. Cut a 2-inch slit along each side edge where you made your mark. Pin the bottom edges of the arms around the finger holes. Sew a whip stitch around the edges of the arms to the glove.

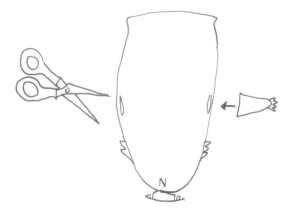

9 Place the mitten thumb side up again. Sew the ears along A–B. Place the ears on the head, adjust them at an angle, and pin them in place. Whip stitch the ears to the head.

10 Place the tail stripes along the glove thumb, about 3/4 inch apart. Pin them in place.

11 Hand sew a whip stitch or running stitch along either the top or bottom edges, or use craft glue to attach the stripes to the thumb.

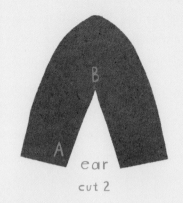

ear
cut 2

hand
cut 2

stripes
cut 2

72

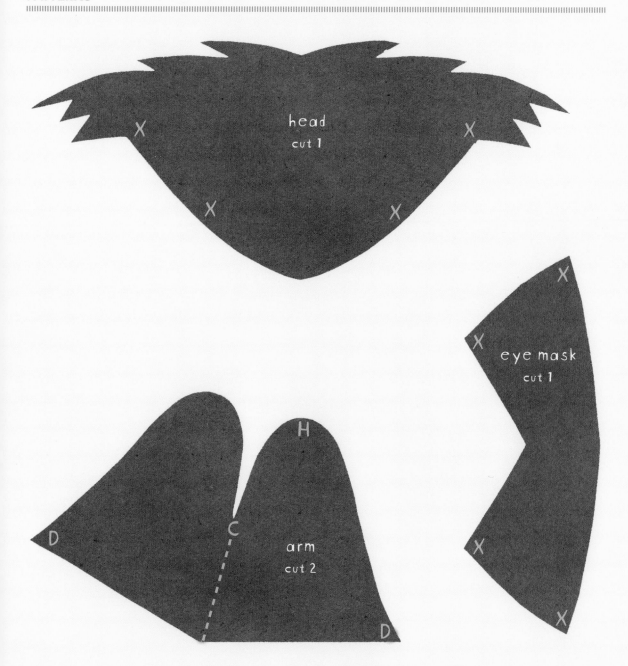

head
cut 1

eye mask
cut 1

arm
cut 2

SUPERHERO MONKEY

LEVEL 1

At lightning fast speed he swings from branch to branch to save his fellow monkeys from trouble. Are you sick from a bushel of bad bananas? He'll bring medicine right over. Is your tail tangled in a knot? He'll get you swinging again in no time. Is your call off? He'll get your cry back in key. If real danger occurs and you're looking into the eyes of a furry beast, just holler. He is known to have sweet-talked jungle cats into opting for veggie meals. Helping one primate at a time, he makes the jungle a more peaceful place.

MATERIALS

REUSED AND RECYCLED
1 brown sock

1 scrap of tan felt

1 scrap of yellow felt

1 small scarf or handkerchief

OTHER FABRIC
1 sheet of medium brown felt

EMBELLISHMENTS
2 rubber washers, 1/2-inch diameter

8 inches of ribbon

CONSTRUCTION MATERIALS AND TOOLS

ruler

fabric scissors

fabric marker or chalk

embroidery needle

sea green embroidery floss

craft glue

sewing needle

brown thread

stuffing

CUT FROM PATTERN

FROM BROWN FELT

1 nose

2 ears shape A

1 chin

2 arms

1 banana stem

FROM TAN FELT

1 eye shape

2 ears shape B

FROM YELLOW FELT

1 banana

INSTRUCTIONS

1 Place the sock flat on your work surface, heel side up. When the sock is placed on your hand the heel area will be on the back.

2 Use a fabric marker or chalk to trace nostril lines on the brown felt nose. Use three strands of the embroidery floss (you'll need to separate the floss to get three strands) to embroider the nostrils following the lines you traced.

3 Align the nose along the toe edge of the sock. Align the eye shape above it. The nose shape should overlap the bottom edge of the eye shape about 1/8 to 1/4 inch. Apply craft glue to back side of the eye shape and press it down onto the sock. Then apply glue to the nose shape and attach it, overlapping the eye shape and sock. Allow the glue to dry before you continue. If you want, you can reinforce the attachment by whip stitching along the felt edge into the top layer of the sock after the glue is dry.

76

4 To make the eyes, apply craft glue to the backs of the rubber washers and place them about 1/2 inch apart onto the eye shape. Press down and allow them to dry before you continue.

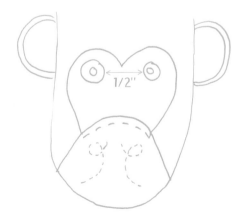

1/2"

5 Apply craft glue to the back of one ear shape A and press it onto one ear shape B. Repeat with the other ear shapes so you have a left and a right ear. Allow the glue to dry before you continue. Use three strands of the embroidery floss to sew a whip stitch or blanket stitch along the curved edge of the ears. Align the ears along the sides on the sock so the top of each ear begins above the top of the eyes. Whip stitch the ears to the sock.

7 Place the arms on either side of the sock about 1 inch below the chin and sew a few whip stitches along the top edges to attach them.

8 Next you need to make a cape for your monkey. Place the handkerchief on your work surface. Take the banana shape and stem shape and either apply glue or hand sew to attach to the cape. Cut the ribbon in half. Sew each ribbon end to either corner of the cape. You can add a dab of craft glue on the edges to keep them from fraying. Allow the glue to dry and then tie the cape around the monkey. Now he is a superhero!

6 Add a handful of stuffing to the head area. Place your hand into the sock so that four fingers go into the head area, and rest your thumb against the front of the sock. You should be able to fold the fabric and make a mouth between your fingers and thumb. Use a fabric marker or chalk to mark the spot on the outside of the sock where your thumb rests. Remove the sock from your hand, lay it flat on your work surface, and glue the chin at the mark.

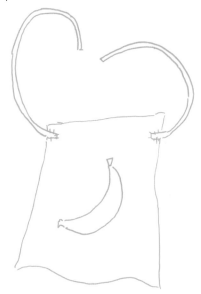

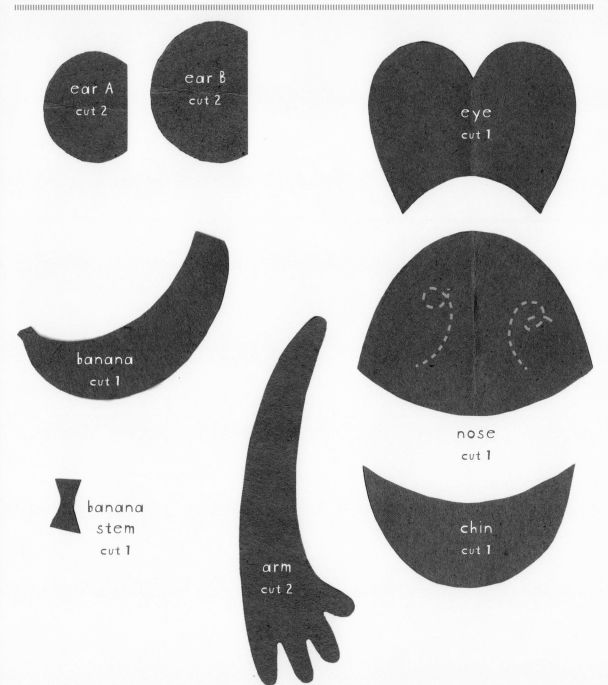

ear A
cut 2

ear B
cut 2

eye
cut 1

banana
cut 1

nose
cut 1

banana
stem
cut 1

arm
cut 2

chin
cut 1

THE FIVE LITTLE PIGS

LEVEL 1

This little pig went to the supermarket to buy bread.

This little pig stayed home sulking.

This little pig had a roast beef on a fresh baguette.

This little pig had zilch!

And this little pig cried, "Boo-hoo-hoo" all the way home.

The origin of this pig rhyme comes from a rental sty occupied by five little pigs. Malcolm Pig had a craving for his favorite pickle-peanut butter and cheese sandwich and went to the supermarket to buy bread. He asked Carl Pig if he wanted to come along, but Carl was lazy and stayed home. Exhausted from grocery shopping Malcolm came back and dozed off before making his sandwich. Shortly after, Vanessa Pig came home hungry from her mud bath. She noticed the fresh bread on the counter and made an enormous roast beef sandwich. Howard Pig asked for a bite but Vanessa would not share, which upset him. Meanwhile a classmate of Violet Pig's remarked that she was neither stinky nor dirty enough to be a proper pig. Violet cried all the way home, waking up Malcolm.

MATERIALS

REUSED AND RECYCLED

1 light pink glove

1 scrap of pink felt

1 scrap of purple felt

1 scrap of black felt

1 scrap of brown felt

1 scrap of white felt

1 scrap of yellow felt

1 scrap of orange felt

1 scrap of red felt

1 scrap of blue felt

EMBELLISHMENTS

8 mini googly eyes

2 long, thin beads

5 miscellaneous round buttons

2 1/2 inches of thin (1/4 inch width) ribbon

CONSTRUCTION MATERIALS AND TOOLS

ruler

fabric scissors

sewing needle

variety of colors of thread (such as pink, white, black, tan, and brown)

craft glue

CUT FROM PATTERN

FROM FELT

1 head each of shapes A, B, C, D, and E, each from different colors of felt

4 ears shape F (colors can be different)

6 ears shape G (colors can be different)

FROM RED

1 meat shape

FROM ORANGE

1 roof

FROM WHITE

2 bags

FROM BROWN

2 bread loaves

FROM YELLOW

1 house

CUT FREEHAND

FROM RED FELT

1 tongue shape

FROM BLACK FELT

small smile shape

small circle mouth shape

FROM BLUE FELT

2 small tears

A
X
B
C
D
E
y

INSTRUCTIONS

1 Align each pair of ears on the back side of a head and whip stitch to attach them.

2 Arrange a pair of googly eyes on each of four heads, the pair of beads for eyes on the Pig D, and buttons for the noses. Use a small amount of craft glue to attach them, and allow the glue to dry before continuing.

3 **Pig A:** Glue the small smile shape to the head. Hand sew head shape A to glove finger A. Place bread loaf shapes together, matching edges, and sew a whip stitch along the edges. Sew lines on the top of the bread with red thread. Whip stitch the bag shapes together, sewing along the curve, leaving the straight side open and unsewn. Sew one end of the ribbon to each side to make a strap for the bag. Place the bread loaf in the bag. Tack the ribbon to the glove at point x.

4 **Pig B:** Use two strands of white thread to embroider a frown for the mouth. Hand sew head shape B to glove finger B. Cut out a window from the square house. Overlap the roof edge along the top edge of the house. Whip stitch across the back to attach the two pieces. Arrange the house so the pig's head fits through the window. Tack the house to the pig's head from the back so the stitches will be hidden.

5 **Pig C:** Use two strands of black thread to embroider a 3/4-inch smile. Whip stitch head shape C to glove finger C. Glue the small red tongue to the mouth to make the pig licking his lips. Glue the meat shape so it is between the bread slices and sticking out of the edge just a little. Tack the sandwich to the glove at point Y with two stitches.

6 **Pig D:** Glue the mouth to the head. Sew the head shape D to glove finger D.

7 **Pig E:** Use two strands of black thread and embroider a wide upside down V-shaped mouth. Sew shape E to glove finger E. Glue tears to the head.

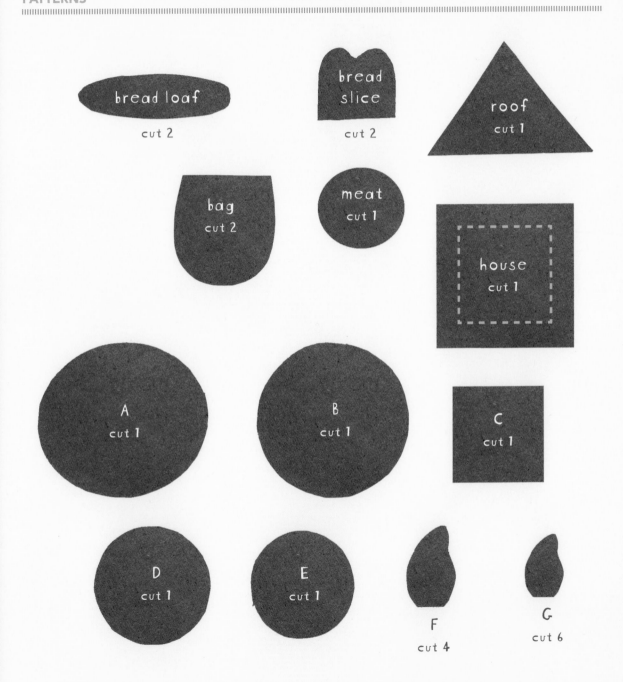

bread loaf
cut 2

bread slice
cut 2

roof
cut 1

bag
cut 2

meat
cut 1

house
cut 1

A
cut 1

B
cut 1

C
cut 1

D
cut 1

E
cut 1

F
cut 4

G
cut 6

TWO-FACED FISH

LEVEL 2

The Two-Faced Fish can be found swimming down a calm river or gliding across a cool lake on a sunny day. However, this finicky aquatic animal can fool you, so don't be deceived if you see him when going for a dip. At first he appears quite friendly, circling around you, but the next minute he becomes fierce, showing some flashy white choppers. Watch out!

MATERIALS

REUSED AND RECYCLED
2 different colored washcloths
(such as turquoise and light green)

1 scrap of cotton print

1 scrap of magenta felt

1 scrap of navy blue felt

1 scrap of white felt

87

CONSTRUCTION MATERIALS AND TOOLS

ruler

fabric scissors

pins

fabric marker or chalk

sewing needle

light green thread

turquoise thread

magenta thread

white thread

craft glue (optional)

CUT FROM PATTERN

FROM TURQUOISE WASHCLOTH
1 fin

1 body

1 eye shape C

FROM LIGHT GREEN WASHCLOTH
1 fin

1 body

1 eye shape C

FROM COTTON PRINT
2 fins (cut 1 in reverse)

FROM MAGENTA FELT
1 mouth

2 eye shapes B

FROM NAVY BLUE FELT
2 eye shapes A

FROM WHITE FELT
2 teeth

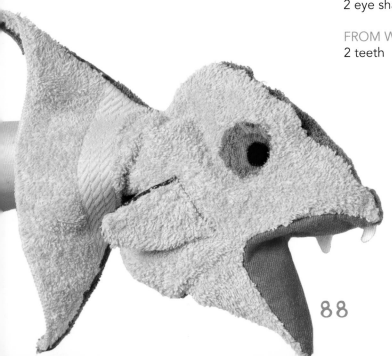

INSTRUCTIONS

1 Place 1 cotton print fin right side down on top of a washcloth fin, matching edges, and pin them together. Whip stitch around the edges, leaving side F unsewn for turning right side out. Repeat with the other fin shapes. Turn each right side out and set aside.

2 Take both body shapes and mark the line from points Y and M. Cut along the line, being careful not to cut past point M. Then place the body shapes together, matching edges, and pin.

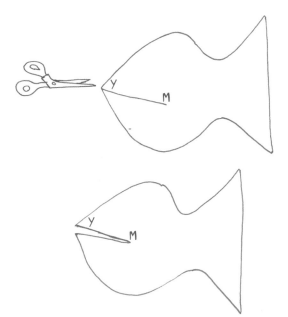

3 Fold the mouth in half and align it along the opening between points Y and M. Pin the mouth in place.

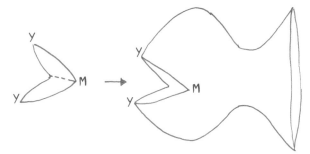

4 Whip stitch along the body with either turquoise or light green thread, leaving the opening between points X and Z unsewn for the hand opening. I find it easiest to sew from X–Y along the bottom and then sew from Y–Z along the top. Then go back and sew along the perimeter of the mouth shape.

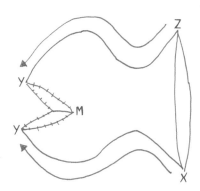

5 Turn the body right side out. Align each fin on either side of the body at points F and F with the cotton print facing in toward the body. Whip stitch fins with matching color thread along side F on the washcloth side and the cotton print side to attach to the body.

6 Place one eye shape A on one eye shape B and hand sew or use glue to attach them. Then place them on eye shape C and sew or glue them together. Finally, place the combined eye shape on the side of the body that is the opposite color of eye C and sew (making sure to only go through the top layer of the fish) or glue to attach them. Repeat with the other eye shapes. You can vary the placement of A and B on C to have the eye looking up, down, or sideways.

7 Choose which side of the fish will have the teeth. Arrange the teeth along the mouth line between points M and Y. Hand sew a few stitches on side T to attach the teeth along the mouth line.

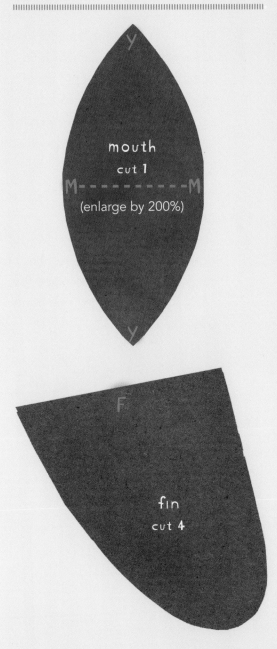

Y

mouth
cut 1
M- - - - - - - - -M
(enlarge by 200%)

Y

F

fin
cut 4

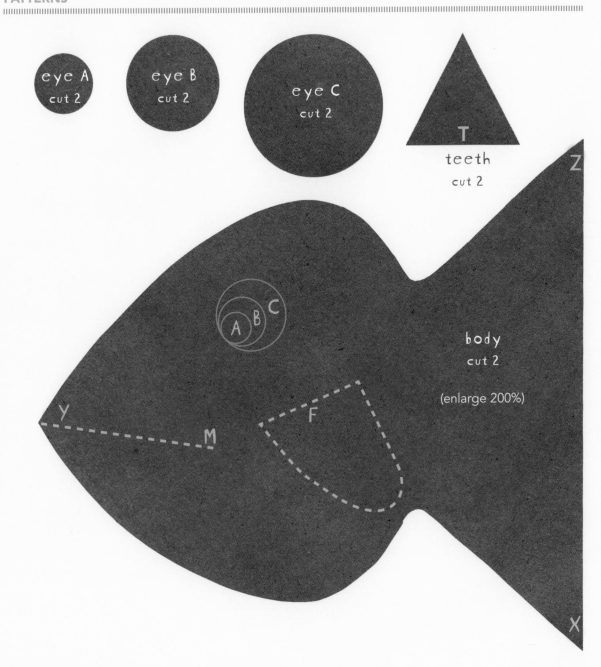

eye A
cut 2

eye B
cut 2

eye C
cut 2

T
teeth
cut 2

Z

A B C

body
cut 2

(enlarge 200%)

Y

M

F

X

TWO BLUE MICE

LEVEL 1

These two sneaky squeaks work as a team to sniff out their favorite cheese. Not just any cheese will satisfy them—only blue cheese. Stilton, roquefort, gorgonzola, and cabrales are just few of the blue cheeses they crave. Their constant diet of blue cheese has turned them from gray to bright blue!

MATERIALS

REUSED AND RECYCLED

1 blue mitten

1 scrap of black felt

OTHER FABRIC

1 sheet of light blue felt

EMBELLISHMENTS

4 black snaps

dental floss or orange embroidery floss

2 light pink pom poms (One can be smaller than the other, or you can use the same size and trim one if needed.)

1 shoelace

CONSTRUCTION MATERIALS AND TOOLS

ruler

fabric scissors

fabric marker

sewing needle

light blue thread

craft glue

CUT FROM PATTERN

FROM LIGHT BLUE FELT

2 ears shape A

2 ears shape B

2 feet shape A

2 feet shape B

CUT FREEHAND

FROM BLACK FELT

1 U-shaped mouth

INSTRUCTIONS

1 For eyes, position the snaps on the thumb and the larger mitten section and use a fabric marker to mark where they should go. If your mitten is knitted, you can push one part of the snap from the back of the mitten and connect the second part on top without glue or sewing. If your mitten is fabric, hand sew the snaps onto the mitten.

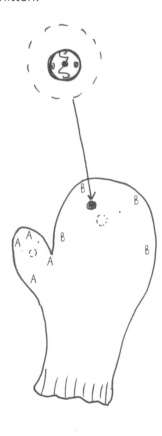

2 Cut three to six full strands of dental or embroidery floss that are 3 inches long and double knot them in the center for mouse A's whiskers. Cut three full strands that are 2 inches long and double knot them in the center for mouse B's whiskers. Use craft glue to attach them to the mitten and allow it to dry before you continue.

3 Apply a small amount of craft glue to each of the pom poms and attach one to mouse A and the other to mouse B where the noses should go.

4 Apply glue to the mouth and attach it to mouse A below the nose.

5 Take each of the ears, pinch the corners together, and sew a few stitches in each to hold in place. Position the large ears on mouse A and the small ears on mouse B and hand sew three stitches in each to attach them.

95

6 Position the big feet on mouse A and the little feet on mouse B and use craft glue to attach them. If you want, you can reinforce the attachment by hand sewing the feet through the top layer of the mitten after the glue is dry.

7 Cut a 6 1/2-inch long shoelace piece for mouse A's tail and a 3 1/3-inch long shoelace piece for mouse B's tail. Put a small amount of craft glue on any cut ends to keep them from fraying. Allow the glue to dry before continuing. Fold one end of each shoelace under 1/4 inch. Hand sew a few stitches on each tail to tack the end down, then sew through the fold and into the back of the mitten at point T.

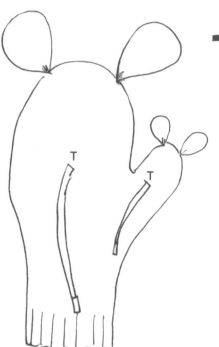

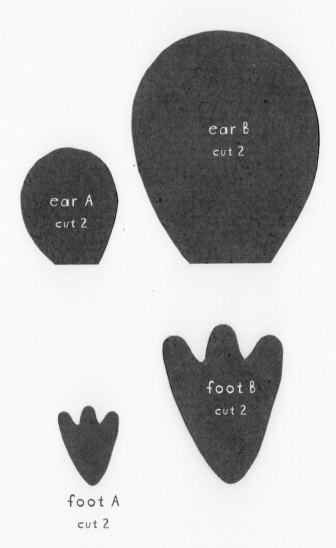

ear A
cut 2

ear B
cut 2

foot B
cut 2

foot A

cut 2

SYLVESTER THE VAMPIRE

LEVEL 2

Sylvester, once a bloodsucker, is now retired because of his gingivitis problems. He has substituted his drink of choice with tomato juice, a less violent and more people-friendly beverage. Sylvester dreams one day a powerful sunscreen will come out that will allow him to enjoy daytime activities. He misses going to the beach and attending baseball games. Sylvester's advice is, "Eat garlic every day. Vampires and friends will probably stay away from you."

MATERIALS

REUSED AND RECYCLED
1 white crew or sweat sock

fabric covering from a broken umbrella or from an umbrella sleeve

1 scrap of faux fur

OTHER FABRIC
2 sheets of black felt

1 sheet of lime green felt

EMBELLISHMENTS
2 googly eyes

pistachio or other small nut shell

CUT FROM PATTERN

FROM UMBRELLA FABRIC
2 cape shapes

1 collar

FROM BLACK FELT
4 wing shapes

1 mustache

FROM LIME GREEN FELT
2 arm shapes

2 fangs

2 ears

FROM FAUX FUR
1 hair shape

CUT FREEHAND

FROM BLACK FELT
2 eye shapes larger than googly eyes

CONSTRUCTION MATERIALS AND TOOLS
ruler

fabric scissors

pins

craft glue

sewing machine (optional)

sewing needle

black thread

lime green thread

INSTRUCTIONS

1 Pin together two wing shapes, matching edges, and whip stitch together with black thread, leaving side X–Y unsewn for a finger opening. Repeat with the other two wing shapes.

2 Use a small amount of craft glue to attach each arm shape to a wing shape so you have one facing left and one facing right. Set aside to dry.

3 Pin together the two cape shapes with wrong sides facing in, matching edges, and machine or hand sew a backstitch or running stitch down the sides from points Y to points Z. Turn the cape right side out.

4 Pin the collar to the cape, C to C. All the corners should also meet, X to X. Machine or hand sew a running stitch to attach them.

5 Place the cape so the collar is facing your work surface. Pin the wings to the cape, X to X, and Y to Y. Whip stitch to attach the front side of the wing to the cape and then the back side to the cape so there is an opening for your finger

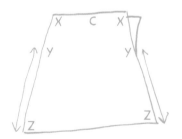

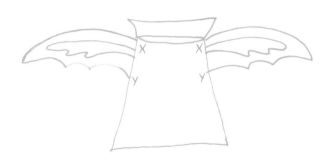

6 Measure about 4 1/2 inches down from the top of the sock. Cut a 1 1/2-inch vertical slit on the left and right sides of the sock for finger holes.

7 Place the ears on the sock. Sew a few stitches with lime green thread through E to attach them.

8 Use craft glue to attach the eye shapes to the sock. Allow the glue to dry before continuing. Then center the googly eyes on top of the eye shapes and attach them with craft glue. Arrange the mustache and fangs, leaving room for the nose, and attach them with craft glue. Glue the pistachio shell for the nose above the middle of the mustache.

9 Place a small amount of craft glue on the back of the hair shape, and press the hair on top of the sock so the point of the hair rests in the front, right between the eyes.

10 Place the cape/wings over the sock.

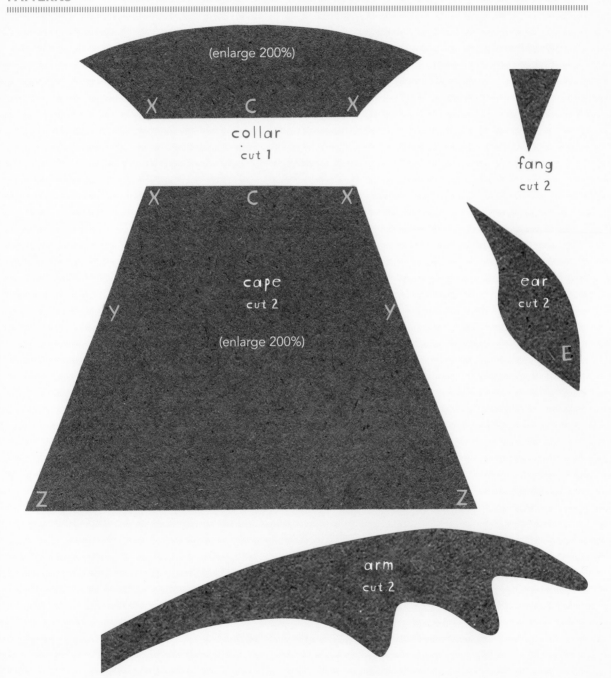

(enlarge 200%)

X C X

collar
cut 1

fang
cut 2

X C X

cape
cut 2

(enlarge 200%)

Y Y

ear
cut 2

E

Z Z

arm
cut 2

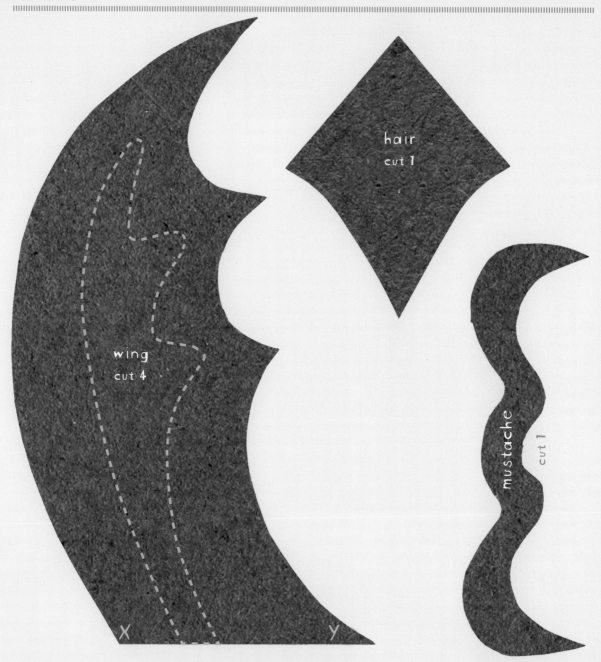

wing
cut 4

hair
cut 1

mustache
cut 1

X

y

BRIAN THE GIRAFFE

LEVEL 3

Brian may appear to be a typical giraffe grazing on the African savanna, spending most of the day under the hot sun. However, take a closer look as he munches on his acacia leaves. Brian, aka the Brain, is an astute spy trained to look out for lions and leopards that may try to eat fellow giraffes. He uses spy binoculars and a security camera in the trees to see high up and over the land.

MATERIALS

REUSED AND RECYCLED
1 yellow dish or tea towel (about 16 x 18 inches)

1 scrap of black felt

OTHER FABRIC
1 sheet of yellow felt

rectangle of brown fleece, 8 x 3 inches

EMBELLISHMENTS

4 wooden old-fashioned clothespins
(the kind without springs)

2 turquoise buttons

1 brown pipe cleaner

1 gift bag rope handle (cut to about 5 1/2 inches)

CONSTRUCTION MATERIALS AND TOOLS

ruler

fabric scissors

pins

sewing machine (optional)

sewing needle

yellow thread

brown thread

craft glue

stuffing

stuffing stick or pencil

CUT FROM PATTERN

FROM DISH TOWEL
2 body shapes (1 cut in reverse)

FROM YELLOW FELT
4 legs

2 heads

1 mouth

FROM BROWN FLEECE
2 ears

FROM BLACK FELT
1 tongue

CUT FREEHAND

FROM BROWN FLEECE
2 tiny triangles

20 to 24 irregularly shaped patches

rectangle, 8 inches x 1/2 inch

INSTRUCTIONS

1 Place the body shapes on your work surface and cut two leg slits on each as indicated. Pin the body shapes right sides together, matching edges, and machine or hand sew them together with a backstitch, leaving the hand opening, side H, unsewn. Set the body aside.

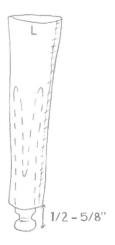

1/2 - 5/8"

106

2 Fold the legs in half lengthwise and whip stitch with yellow thread down the sides only, leaving the top open. Place a small amount of craft glue on each clothespin and gently slide it into a felt leg, small tip down, through opening L. Push all the way down until the clothespin sticks out of the bottom about 1/2 to 5/8 inch.

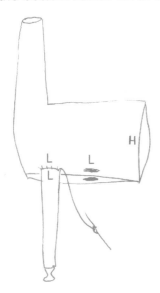

3 Whip stitch the edge of the leg opening to the edge of the slit on the body, from points L to L, making sure the leg seams face the side where the hand opening is.

4 Pin the head shapes together, matching edges, and whip stitch around them with yellow thread, leaving side Y unsewn. Place the tongue on the mouth and hand sew two stitches at point T. Then sew a few stitches on either side of the mouth to attach it to the bottom of the head.

5 Pinch the corners of the ears to gather them. Place them on the head, E to E, and sew a few stitches with brown thread to attach them.

6 Apply craft glue on the tiny triangles and attach them to the head at point N for nostrils. Allow the glue to dry before continuing.

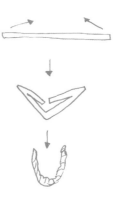

7 Arrange the buttons on the head for eyes and sew to attach.

8 To make horns, cut 4 inches from a pipe cleaner and fold each end in toward the center. Twist both sides and curl the pipe cleaner into a U-shape. Cut a tiny slit on each side at the top of the head and slip the pipe cleaner horns through the slits.

9 Place the head on the body, Y to Y, and whip stitch the edges with yellow thread.

10 Apply a small amount of craft glue to the wrong sides of the brown patches and press them onto the body fabric. Allow the glue to dry before continuing. If you want, you can hand sew a few stitches around each patch for extra reinforcement.

11 Use the fleece rectangle to make a mane by cutting slits along one side for a fringed look. Beginning at point M on the head and continuing all the way down, whip stitch with brown thread to attach the mane to the neck.

12 Make a tail from the gift bag rope. First make a knot at one end. Place the knot on the inside of the hand opening at point Z. Hand sew three or four stitches through the knot to attach the tail. Then knot the tail at the opposite end.

13 Push small amounts of stuffing into the neck so it stands upright, using a stuffing stick or

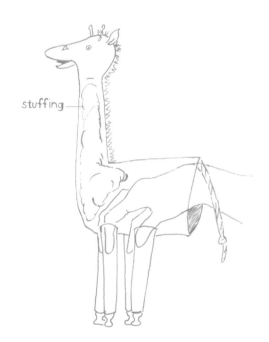

stuffing

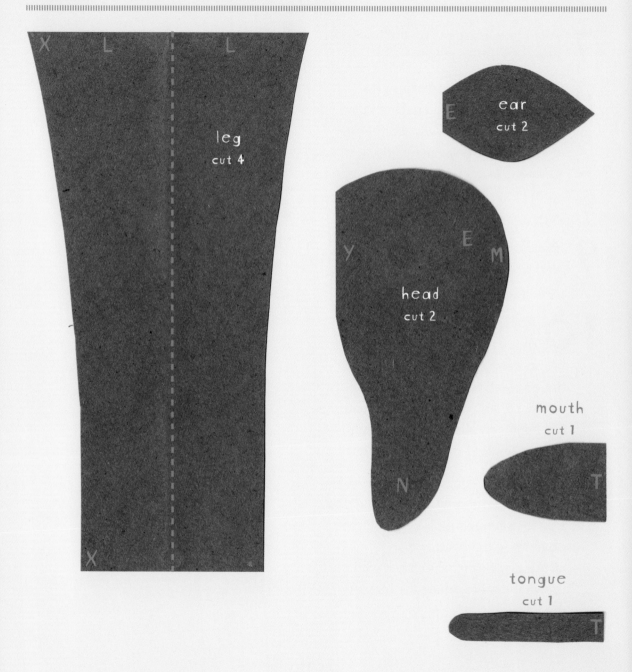

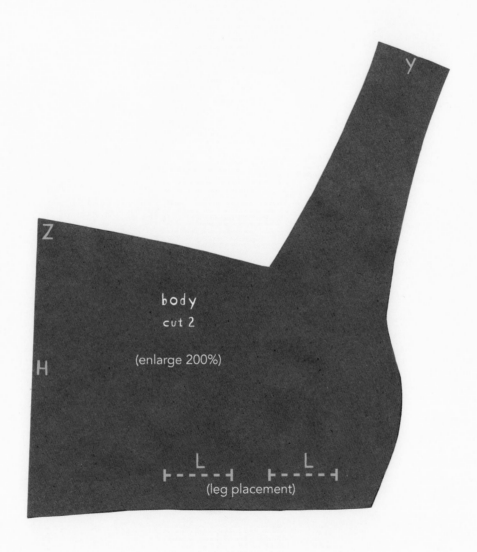

Y

Z

body
cut 2

(enlarge 200%)

H

L   L
(leg placement)

THE ARTIST

LEVEL 2

Bernard's passion is painting. He paints *en plein air* in the petite garden behind his apartment, in the meadow of the park, along the bridge overlooking the river, or by the market filled with wonderful food. His colorful paintings are highly regarded by art critics as the *crème de la crème*.

"Bernard sees not only what we don't, in the ordinary, but what we should," said a recent gallery owner raving about his work.

MATERIALS

REUSED AND RECYCLED
1 old stained t-shirt or other light-colored shirt

1 scrap of red felt

1 scrap of sage green felt

OTHER FABRIC
1 sheet of black felt

EMBELLISHMENTS
variety of colors of acrylic paint

1 (7- to 8-inch) piece of plastic coated picture hanging wire*

2 beads

1 (8-inch) zipper

art supplies for the artist bag (small paint brush, pencil, paint tubes)

white card stock

button and/or decoration for the artist bag

*Plastic-coated wire works better because the ends won't be as sharp when cut.

CONSTRUCTION MATERIALS AND TOOLS

ruler

fabric scissors

paper scissors

newspaper

paint brush

pins

sewing machine (optional)

sewing needle

white thread

black thread

wire cutters (optional)

embroidery needle

embroidery floss (contrasting color)

craft glue

stuffing

CUT FROM PATTERN

FROM T-SHIRT
2 body shapes**

FROM BLACK FELT
2 front vests (If your felt is embossed, cut 1 front vest in reverse.)

1 back vest

2 beret shapes

FROM SAGE GREEN FELT
2 artist bag shapes

FROM CARD STOCK
1 artist palette

CUT FREEHAND

FROM RED FELT
1 ring-shaped mouth

**(It's helpful to use the existing seams of the t-shirt for the bottoms of the body shapes, the arm sleeve opening, so you don't have to sew a seam there.)

INSTRUCTIONS

1 Before beginning, you may want to put newspaper down to protect your work surface. Place the body shapes right side up on your work surface. Use light brush strokes to sporadically apply colorful paint on both body shapes. Too much paint will soak through the fabric and take longer to dry, so don't load your brush with paint. Allow the paint to dry before continuing.

2 Pin the body shapes right sides together, matching edges, and machine or hand sew with white thread a backstitch or running stitch about 1/4 inch from the edges, leaving the hand opening unsewn. Turn the body right side out.

3 To make the glasses, curl and bend the plastic-coated wire into one loop and then a second loop, with about 1/4 inch between them and about 1/4 inch on each side. Shape the glasses to fit the face and place them on the head. Sew a few stitches on each side of the glasses to attach them to the face.

4 Sew the beads with black thread inside the glasses for eyes. Remove the zipper pull from the fabric strips and teeth. Be careful—you may need wire cutters to separate it from the teeth. Place the teeth strips aside. Place the zipper pull on the face to make a nose. Either sew a few stitches through the hole or use craft glue to attach it. Then apply craft glue on the back of the mouth and attach it. Allow the glue to dry before you continue.

5 Pin the front vest shapes to the back vest shape right sides together, matching points V to V, and whip stitch down the sides with black thread. Then sew the top of the vest pieces, along side X, to attach them. Turn the vest right side out and pull the puppet's arms through the arm holes.

6 Pin both beret shapes together. Sew a whip stitch with black thread around the outside, leaving about a 1-inch opening unsewn. Place a pinch of stuffing through the opening to give the beret some shape and whip stitch to close the opening. Cut about 1 inch of the fabric strip from the zipper and sew it at the center top of the beret so it sticks up a little. Use the other fabric strip, with the teeth still attached, to make a brim for the beret. Form an oval shape with the zipper strip so that the fabric side faces into the beret. Pin it in place and hand sew a whip stitch around the edges of the zipper fabric to attach it to the felt. Set the beret aside.

7 To make the artist bag, pin both felt bag shapes together. Use three strands of embroidery floss (you'll need to separate the floss to get three strands) to sew a blanket stitch along the outside edge. Use the remaining piece of zipper fabric to make a strap. Stitch the opposite ends to the inside of the artist bag at points Y. Place some art supplies inside the bag.

8 Turn the card stock shape into a paint palette by simply painting a few color spots on it. *Magnifique!*

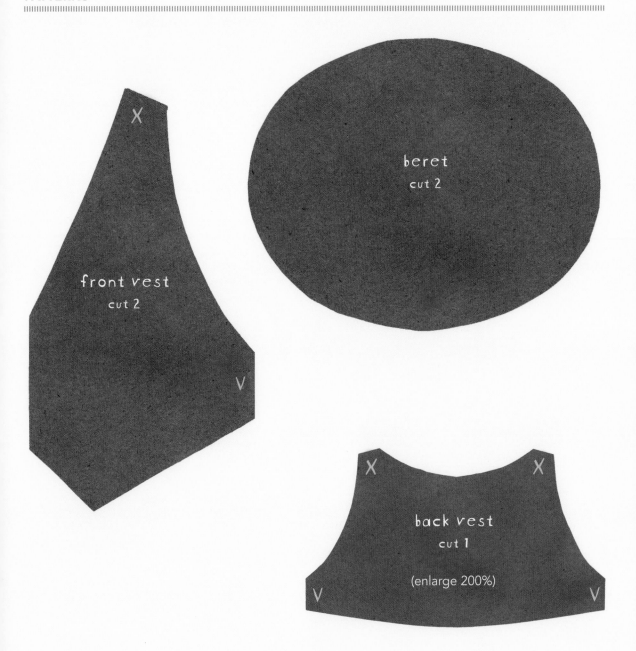

front vest
cut 2

beret
cut 2

back vest
cut 1

(enlarge 200%)

artist bag
cut 2

Y   Y

artist palette
cut 1

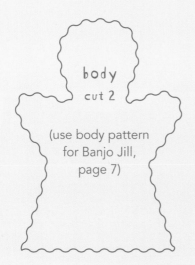

body
cut 2

(use body pattern
for Banjo Jill,
page 7)

BEAN-BOT

LEVEL 3

Bean-Bot's parents were a can of garbanzo beans and a can of lima beans. After his parents' sudden disappearance one day after lunch, Bean-Bot found himself alone and in great risk of being sent to the crusher. A kind boy picked him out and brought him home, transforming him into a robot. Although he has been programmed to do arduous tasks such as washing laundry, walking the dog, and homework, he also enjoys showing off his dance moves at parties.

Note: This project is advanced and uses sharp metal objects, hardware, and tools. This should be done with an older child and with close adult supervision. The cans should be washed thoroughly. Watch for any sharp edges where the lid was attached.

119

MATERIALS

REUSED AND RECYCLED
4 old notebook wire spirals or springs

2 keys

1 large aluminum can (approximately 28-ounce size), emptied and cleaned, label removed, lids discarded

1 small aluminum can (approximately 15-ounce size), emptied and cleaned, label removed, lids discarded

large button or bead

2 rulers (or 12-inch wooden dowels)

EMBELLISHMENTS
2 large metal nuts (1-inch diameter or larger, and should have weight)

1 to 2 shoelaces, depending on the length

1 thimble

2 key covers

1 twist tie

2 small (refrigerator light–size) light bulbs (optional)

1 metal drain catch (optional)

1 small binder clip (optional)

OTHER FABRIC
1 sheet of purple felt

CONSTRUCTION MATERIALS AND TOOLS
2 feet of copper wire

wire cutters

pliers

4 jump rings

marker

awl, or hammer and nail

8 inches of jewelry wire

hot glue gun

fabric scissors

12 1/2 feet of clear fishing line or thread

masking tape

1 Begin by making the legs and feet. Use the wire cutters to cut a piece of copper wire about 8 inches long. Wrap the end of the wire through one nut (the foot), loop it around one side, and twist it together until tight. You can use the pliers to help tighten the wire. Then wrap the wire through the center and around one side of the nut four times. Use the pliers to tighten one end of a notebook spiral into a closed loop. Wrap the copper wire through the loop in the notebook spiral a few times to attach it to the nut, and then pull the copper wire back through the nut. Loop the copper wire around the other side of the nut a few times, then around the spiral loop a few more times, until the two are securely attached. Use the wire cutters to trim any excess copper wire. Repeat for the second leg. Slide one jump ring onto the opposite end of each leg. You will need to tighten the spiral loop so the jump ring does not shift. Set the legs aside.

2 You will use the remaining two wire spirals and the two keys to make the arms and hands. Take one end of a wire spiral and use pliers to make the loop smaller and close it into a circle. Use the wire cutters to cut 4 inches of copper wire. Pull the copper wire through the hole in the key and then through the closed spiral loop. Wrap the copper wire through several times until the key is secure, using pliers if necessary to tighten it. Repeat for the second arm. Slide one jump ring onto the opposite end of each arm and tighten the spiral as before. Set the arms aside.

3 The larger can will be the body. Use a marker to make two dots along the edge of the can and one at the top center, as shown. Carefully use the awl (or a hammer and nail) to poke all three holes. Next, punch a fourth hole through the center top of the smaller can, which becomes the head.

4 Preheat your hot glue gun while you do this step. Use the wire cutters to cut a piece of jewelry wire about 8 inches long. Thread the jewelry wire from the outside of the can through one of the holes you punched in the sides, then through both leg jump rings, then through the other hole to the outside of the can, as shown. Pull on the ends of the jewelry wire until an equal amount is hanging out each side of the can, then loop each end around the rim of the can, and twist them around the wire inside the can. Use pliers to twist and tighten the wires, which will keep the jump rings from sliding too much. Trim the ends of the wire as needed.

5 Apply a small amount of hot glue at the center back of the can and press the shoelace onto it. Continue to apply hot glue in a line around the can, gluing the shoelace down as you go. When you reach the spot where an arm should be, stop and feed the shoelace through one of the arm jump rings. Leave a 1-inch area unglued through the jump ring so it is loose against the can, and then continue gluing the shoelace around the can, stopping directly across from the arm you just attached. Attach the second arm as you did the first. Finish gluing the shoelace around the can and trim off the excess at the back. Set the body aside.

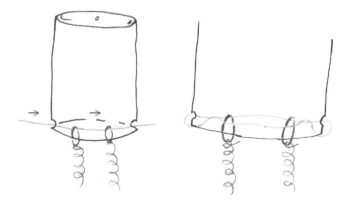

124

6 Use fabric scissors to cut a piece of felt that is long enough and wide enough to cover the small can. (For example, I used a strip for a 15-ounce can that was 1 1/2 inches wide x approximately 7 inches long.) Begin at the center back of the can and apply a small amount of hot glue. Press down the edge of the felt and wrap it around the can, applying glue as you go. Apply a little hot glue to the inside edge of the thimble and press it down on the front of the felt to make the nose. Glue on the key covers to make the eyes. Form the twist tie into an oval. Apply a dot of glue on either side of the twist tie and press it onto the felt to make an asymmetrical mouth.

7 To make the ears, cut two strips of purple felt that are 3/4 inch wide x 2 1/4 inches long. Apply hot glue around the socket end of a light bulb and wrap the felt around it. There should be 1/4 inch of felt sticking out past the edge of the socket end. Apply a small amount of hot glue around the rim of the felt edge and gently press it onto the side of the head, making sure the felt doesn't fold out or under, and holding it until the glue dries. Repeat with the other light bulb. Set the head aside.

8 Use the drain catch to make the hat. Use a little hot glue to attach the remaining shoelace to the back of the catch and wrap it around, gluing as you go, until the ends meet. Trim off any excess shoelace. Attach the binder clip to the shoelace by clipping it on.

9 Finally, make your puppet controls. Cut five pieces of fishing line, each approximately 30 inches long. Bring one through a button or bead and

knot a few times. This will be your stopper. Feed the loose end of the line through the holes in the center of the body and head, then through the center of the hat. Wrap the loose end of the line around the middle of one of the rulers, tie it tightly, and wrap masking tape around to secure it. Tie a second piece of fishing line around the middle of the left leg spiral. Dab a little hot glue on the knot to secure it to the spiral. Pull up the fishing line, but keep the puppet's leg in a straight position. Tie the loose end of the line to the left side of the ruler and secure it with tape. Repeat the process to attach a third line to the right leg and the right end of the ruler. Tie the fourth fishing line left around the key and secure the knot with a little hot glue, pull up the line (keeping the arm relaxed), and tie it around the left side of the second ruler. Secure it with tape. Repeat the process with the fifth and final fishing line, attaching it to the right arm and the right side of the ruler.

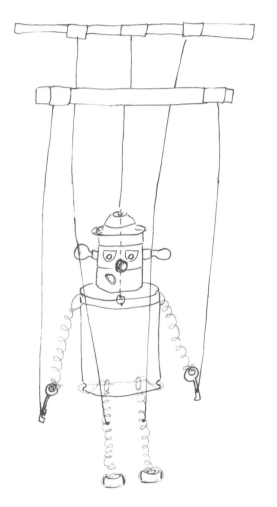

CAPTAIN HOTHEAD THE PIRATE

LEVEL 3

Captain Hothead was once a man filled with fury. He attacked ships, stole treasure, and held ladies hostage all on the high seas. He was a ruthless captain, screaming and punishing his crew. He may have lost a leg from a shark attack, but he never lost his mean streak. Eventually his crew declared mutiny, took over the ship, and left him alone on an island. Now he is left to complain to the birds about his sunburn.

MATERIALS

REUSED AND RECYCLED

1 scrap of black felt

1 scrap of brown ultrasuede or cotton fabric

1 scrap of gray felt

1 dental floss container

1 popsicle stick

2 mismatched gloves

1 old-fashioned wooden clothespin

1 striped sock

1 cardboard toilet paper roll

1 piece of metallic paper (I used a scrap from a takeout carton lid)

1 key

1 scrap of paper, 1/2 inch x 1 1/2 inches

scrap of cotton (can be a patch similar to the Punk Rocker project)

127

OTHER FABRIC
1 sheet of red felt

EMBELLISHMENTS
1 small googly eye

1 small pom pom

2 buttons

ribbon

1 hair elastic

CONSTRUCTION MATERIALS AND TOOLS
ruler

fabric scissors

paper scissors

hot glue gun

pencil

black embroidery floss

red permanent marker

pins

sewing machine (optional)

sewing needle

brown thread

black thread

green thread

red thread (optional)

craft glue

CUT FROM PATTERN

FROM BLACK FELT
1 heel

FROM BROWN FABRIC
2 vest shapes

FROM RED FELT
2 boot shapes A

1 boot shape B

1 boot shape C

FROM GRAY FELT
1 sole

1 heel

2 hat shapes

FROM METALLIC PAPER
2 sword shapes

2 hook shapes

CUT FREEHAND

FROM BLACK FELT
1 circle slightly larger than the googly eye

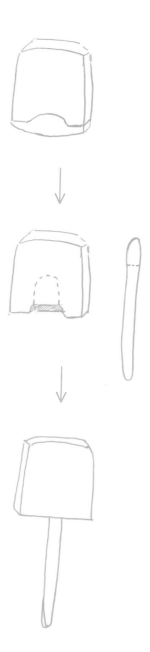

1 Preheat your hot glue gun. Start by making the head. Snap the lid off of the dental floss container. Apply hot glue along 1 1/2 inches of the popsicle stick and press down on the front of the dental floss container to cover the text. On the other side that has no writing, mark with a pencil where the eyes, nose, and mouth will go. Cut a 6-inch piece of embroidery floss. Apply a dot of hot glue where one of the eyes should be on the dental floss container closer to the top, press the floss down, and then place the eye patch on top. Tie a knot in the embroidery floss at the back where the popsicle stick is on the container. Apply a drop of hot glue next to the patch for the other eye and place the black felt circle. Add another drop of hot glue on the felt, and press on the googly eye. Glue on the pom pom in the center of the floss container, below the eyes for a nose. Draw a mouth with permanent marker. Set the head aside.

2 Pin both vest shapes right sides together, matching edges. Using brown thread, machine sew a 1/4-inch seam or hand sew a backstitch or whip stitch along line X–Y. Sew the buttons on the right side of the fabric on one side of the vest and set it aside.

3 You will use your pointer and middle finger to control the pirate's legs with one hand. Cut off three of the fingers from one glove, making sure to use one of the sides so you only have to sew up one side. For example,

either cut off the thumb, pointer, and middle fingers; or the pinky, ring, and middle fingers (shown here). Set the cut-off fingers aside for use on the arms. Turn the glove wrong side out and sew a whip stitch to close the cut side. Turn the glove right side out. The pirate's legs will be asymmetrical, with the peg leg on the longer finger. Cut a tiny hole at the end of that finger hole. Apply hot glue around the top 3/4 of the clothespin and place it into the leg opening. Set the legs aside.

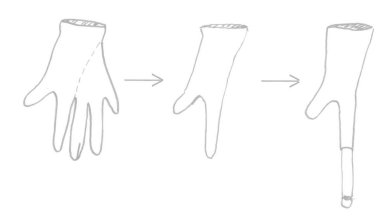

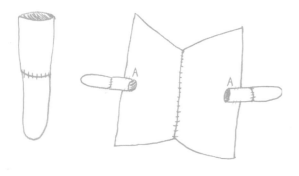

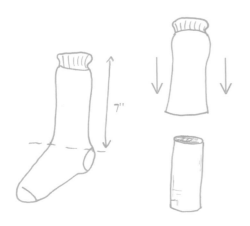

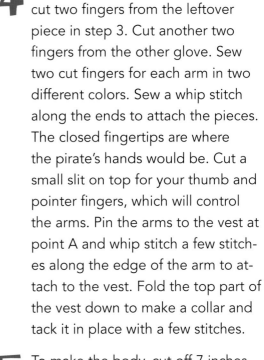

4 To make the pirate's two-tone arms, cut two fingers from the leftover piece in step 3. Cut another two fingers from the other glove. Sew two cut fingers for each arm in two different colors. Sew a whip stitch along the ends to attach the pieces. The closed fingertips are where the pirate's hands would be. Cut a small slit on top for your thumb and pointer fingers, which will control the arms. Pin the arms to the vest at point A and whip stitch a few stitches along the edge of the arm to attach to the vest. Fold the top part of the vest down to make a collar and tack it in place with a few stitches.

5 To make the body, cut off 7 inches from the top of the sock. Place the sock over the cardboard tube and then wrap the vest around it. Wrap the ribbon twice around the middle for a belt and tie a knot in the front.

6 Next, attach the body to the leg opening. Begin at the edge of the glove's opening used for the legs and pin the base of the body to the legs on the front side, tucking the sock fabric edge under. Sew a whip stitch with black thread to attach the two pieces, and set the body/legs aside.

7 To make the swashbuckler pirate boot, pin two boot shapes A together, matching edges, and whip stitch with red or brown thread lengthwise along side S–S. Place boot shape B along the top so the ends S meet along the center back and whip stitch to attach. Fold the top down. Pin boot shape C so that it meets B to B. Sew to attach. Pin the corners of the shoe sole at points T and T and sew around to attach. Place the heel on the boot, matching points H to H, and sew to attach. Thread a sewing needle with a 14-inch double strand of green thread. Insert your needle and pull it most of the way through, leaving 2 inches of thread hanging. Sew a

body

legs

cross-stitch (beginning at the top and going back up) along the front of the boot. Then tie the thread into a bow to finish the laces. Cut off the remaining thread. Place the boot over the other leg and tack with stitches, if needed.

8 To make the hat, pin both hat shapes together, matching edges, and sew along side D–E. Pin the cotton patch on the center front of the hat and whip stitch around the edges to attach it. Place the hat on the head.

9 Apply a few dots of hot glue to the other end of the popsicle stick holding the head and place the popsicle stick into the top of the body opening, between the layer of cardboard and the sock material. Press down.

10 To make the sword, place a few dots of hot glue on the backs of each sword shape. Place the key between the paper layers and press down. Apply a few drops of hot glue on the paper scrap and wrap it around the edge of the key sandwiched between the metallic paper. Cut the hair elastic, pull an end through the hole in the key, and double knot it. Tie the elastic around the arm.

11 Place glue on one side of the hook shape and place the flat side on the tip of the arm. Then add glue to the other side of the hook shape and press together so the arm is sandwiched between both sides of the hook.

boot A
cut 2

boot C
cut 1

heel
cut 1

sole
cut 1

hat
cut 2

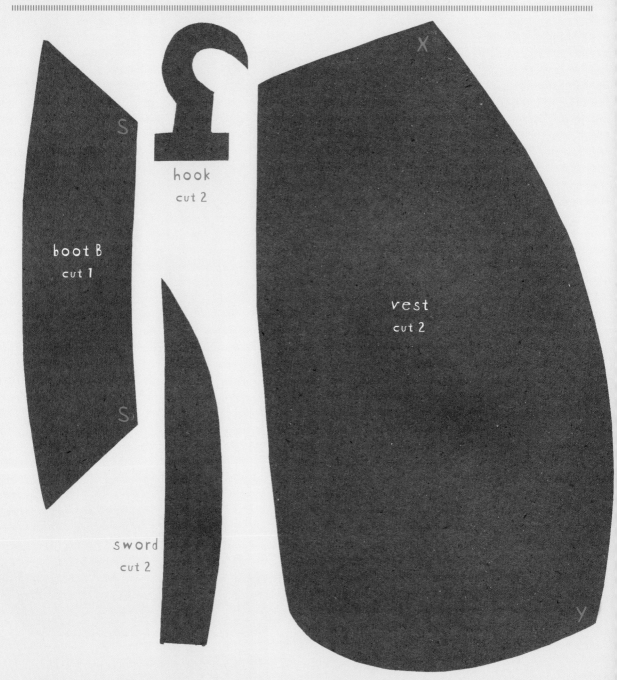

S

hook
cut 2

boot B
cut 1

S

X

vest
cut 2

sword
cut 2

Y

DERZINK THE WIZARD

LEVEL 1

Derzink the Semi-Omniscient is considered by many in the magic realm to be a kvetch. He is often knocking on his wizard friend's doors looking for his misplaced wand. If you fly in for a visit without forewarning him, he will send a wind to blow you away. Try to borrow a book from his library and he'll constantly remind you to not crumple the pages. If you ask to trade magic ingredients, be careful, because he often confuses hog snot with dragon ooze. Derzink gripes that his crystal ball is always too cloudy and needs cleaning, but the other wizards tell him he just needs new glasses.

137

MATERIALS

REUSED AND RECYCLED

2 mismatched socks

1 scrap of yellow felt

1 scrap of white or gray faux fur

EMBELLISHMENTS

5 gold sequins

pencil cap eraser

2 blue sequins

metal ring shapes, about 3/4 inch diameter
(bottlecaps could also be used or pipe
cleaners can be twisted into circles)

yellow acrylic paint

CONSTRUCTION MATERIALS AND TOOLS

ruler

fabric scissors

pins

sewing machine (optional)

sewing needle

thread in a color to match the sock

black thread

yellow thread

fabric marker or chalk

craft glue

pinch of stuffing

CUT FROM PATTERN

FROM YELLOW FELT

1 star

FROM FAUX FUR

1 beard

1 mustache

1 eyebrow

FROM SOCK

2 hats

H

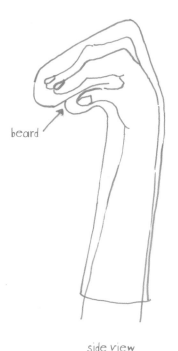

beard

side view

INSTRUCTIONS

1 Start by making the hat. Pin the hat pieces together and machine or hand sew a running stitch along the diagonals. Leave side H open for attaching the hat to the head.

2 Place the star on the hat and either use craft glue or hand sew with yellow thread around the felt to attach it to the hat. Sew gold sequins to the front of the hat, and set it aside.

3 Place the other sock on your hand and close your fingers against your thumb to make a mouth. Use a fabric marker or chalk to mark where your thumb presses against the sock. This is where you will attach the beard. Pin the beard in place with black thread and sew it to the sock along line B–B.

4 Place the sock on your work surface and fold the front forward to meet the beard. Sew or glue in place the mustache right along the toe edge of the sock at point M. Apply craft glue to the back of the eraser and place the tip side down on top of the mustache at the center.

5 Arrange the blue sequins for eyes and sew them to the sock. Place the metal ring shape circles over the sequins for glasses. Sew a few stitches on either side of each metal piece to attach it to the sock.

6 Place the eyebrow above the eyes and either glue or sew to attach it.

7 Place stuffing inside the hat and place the hat on the puppet's head. Sew a few stitches at the sides and front to keep the hat in place.

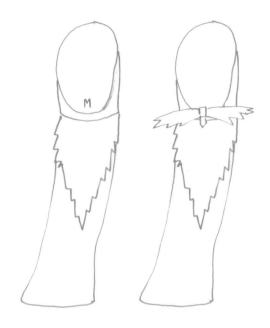

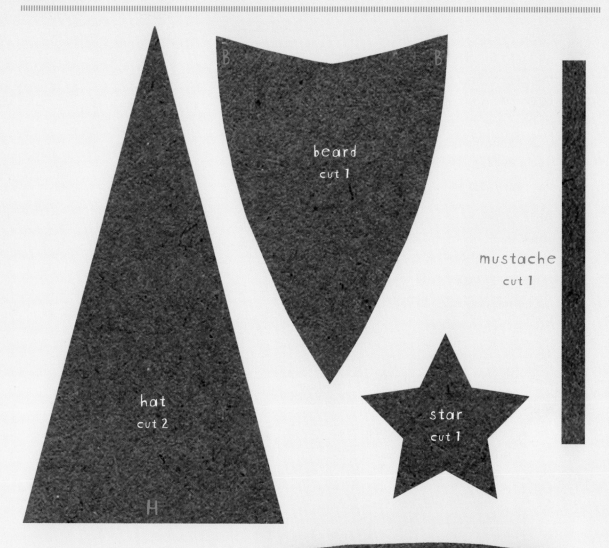

beard
cut 1

mustache
cut 1

hat
cut 2

star
cut 1

eyebrow
cut 1

PLAY

Playing allows your imagination to run wild —and experience the world with your own eyes, ears, fingers, and hands!

Puppets are the perfect toy for playing because they are colorful and tactile. You can use puppets to practice role playing, developing characters, and storytelling. You can also create a unique world for your puppets to live in.

PUPPET THEATER

Now that you have created a plethora of puppets, it's time to perform with them. First, you will need a puppet theater. Make a simple theater with the following materials:

large cardboard box (such as an
   appliance or shipping box)
curtain (old velvet curtain, shower
   curtain, bed sheet, or other fabric)
wooden dowel that is slightly longer
   than the width of the box
utility knife*

paint and paint brushes
   or colored paper
tassel or ribbon (optional)
sewing machine (optional)
thread
needle

*Children should ask for an adult to help when cutting with a utility knife.

Puppet
Play

INSTRUCTIONS

1. Use a pencil to draw a window, making sure to leave about a 3-inch border to the edge. Then use a utility knife to cut out the window, being careful not to cut yourself with the sharp blade.

2. Cut a small hole on each side of the window for a dowel to go through and hold the curtain.

3. Paint the outside of the box a solid color or add decorative details. You can also cover it with colored paper.

4. You will need two sides so you can open up the curtain from the middle to the sides on the stage. If your curtain already has a space at the top for a curtain rod, push the dowel through the top of the curtain. If you use a bed sheet or other fabric, cut it in half so there are two sides to the curtain. If your curtain does not have a fold at the top, fold the top over a couple of inches and machine sew a straight seam so the dowel can fit easily through the hole.

5. Tie the tassel around the bottom of the curtain to keep the fabric gathered.

6. Place the puppet theater high up on a table so the performers can puppeteer and not be seen on the stage.

146

PERFORMANCE TIPS FOR THE PUPPETEER

Practice by manipulating your puppet in front of a mirror. Try moving your hand and fingers in different directions to see how you can make your puppet move. Can your puppet run, dance, jump, skip, fall, and slide? How does one puppet move and interact with another puppet? Three puppets?

After experimenting with movement, try different voices for your puppet's character. The puppet's voice adds a distinct personality. Perhaps your raccoon has a sweet and shy voice. Or your vampire speaks low and muffled or raspy. What does a mechanical robot sound like? Voice projection is also important. Be loud and articulate so your audience can hear you well.

PUTTING ON A PUPPET SHOW

There are several things to consider before you put on a puppet show. What should your show be about? You could try a new twist on a classic fairy tale. Or you could write an exciting and entirely new and never-been-told story. Decide whether the puppet play is serious or humorous. Is there singing or music?

First decide what the plot is. You may need to answer a few questions.

- What is the main problem that occurs?

- What are the main actions that occur with the characters?

- What characters are in the play?

- Where does the story take place?

You may want to improvise the play or write a full script. If you write a script you should include character dialogue. Know your character. Before you get started, answer these questions for each character:

- What is your puppet's name?

- Where does he/she live?

- What does he/she like to eat?

- Who are his/her friends and enemies?

- What hobbies does he/she have?

- How would you describe the puppet's personality?

Decide whether your play needs outdoor lighting or if it can be performed indoors. Do you want music? You can pick recorded music to be played aloud during your show. Are there any special sound effects needed, such as a slamming door, rain falling, or animal sounds? Will the set need a painted backdrop? Paper, illustration board, and cardboard can be painted on to make a set. Acrylic paints are safe and easy to use, and they come in all kinds of colors. Do you need any props? Like your puppets, props can also be made with fabric, cardboard, paper, paint, and objects you find around the house. Just use your imagination!

HOST A PUPPET PARTY

Puppetry is more fun with more people! Host a puppet crafting extravaganza and invite friends and family over to make new puppets and perform with them. Have each guest bring a found object. Also ask each person to write down a puppet character on a piece of paper. Draw names from a hat and create the puppet you choose. Pick a found object from the group and turn it into your puppet. You can also team up with a partner and build the puppet together. It's a great way to work together and share your creative ideas.

149

PUPPET-MAKING RESOURCES

Do you want to learn more about puppetry arts? Get involved and check out these Web sites for more information.

www.bimp.uconn.edu
The Ballard Institute and Museum of Puppetry. A museum dedicated to Puppetry Arts.

www.breadandpuppet.org
Puppet performance and political theater in Vermont.

www.hensonfoundation.org
A great resource for puppet news and performances shown locally and across the United States.

www.puppet.org
Center for Puppetry Arts includes information on the museum and performances.

www.nationalpuppetryfestival.org
A unique puppet festival held in Georgia every two years.

www.puppeteers.org
A Web site that lists events and festivals. Magazine subscription.